AF496645

Alexey Khomych   Hennady Malamed

My Wondrous World

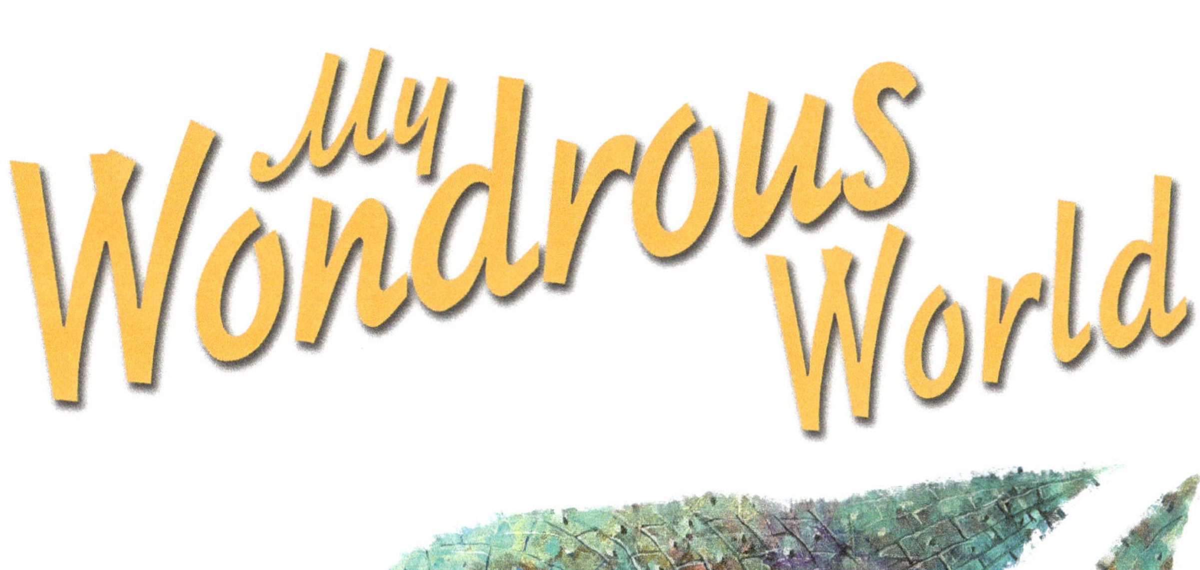

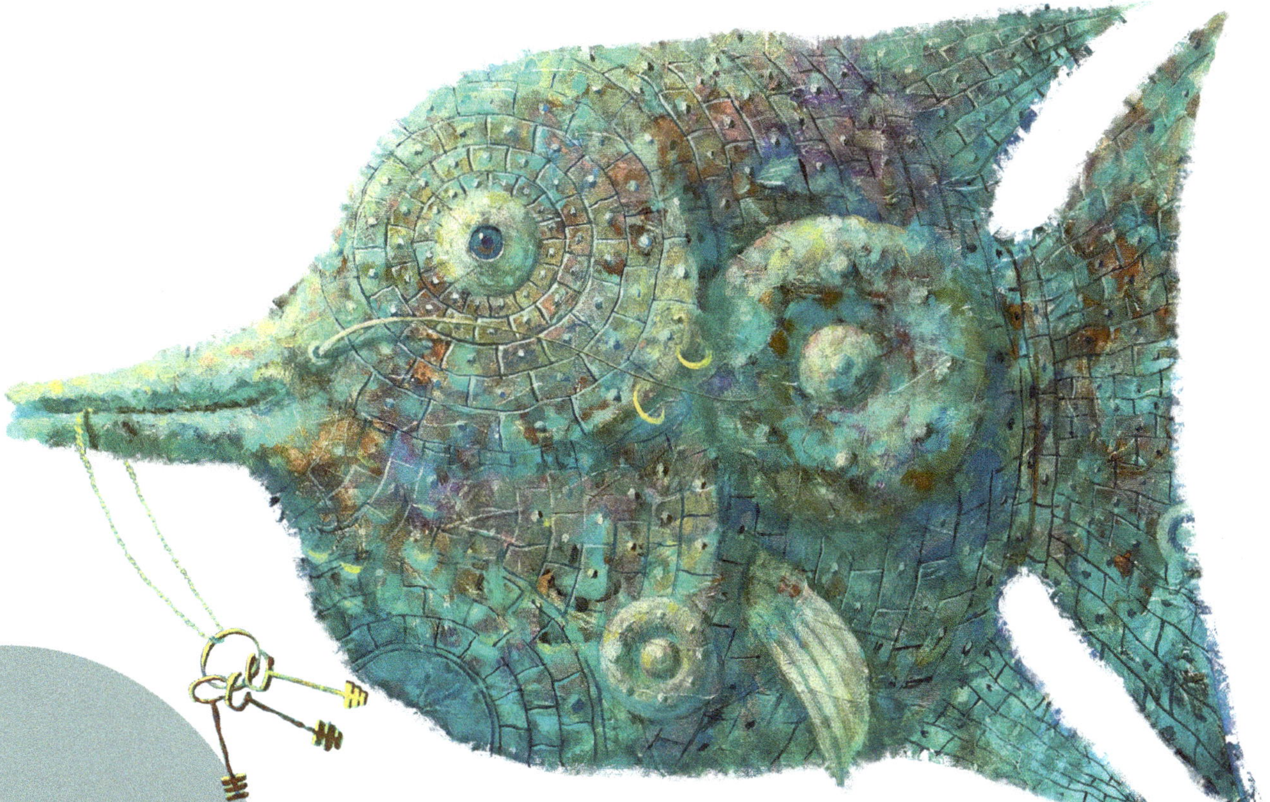

MAGE
Publishing House Ranok Limited

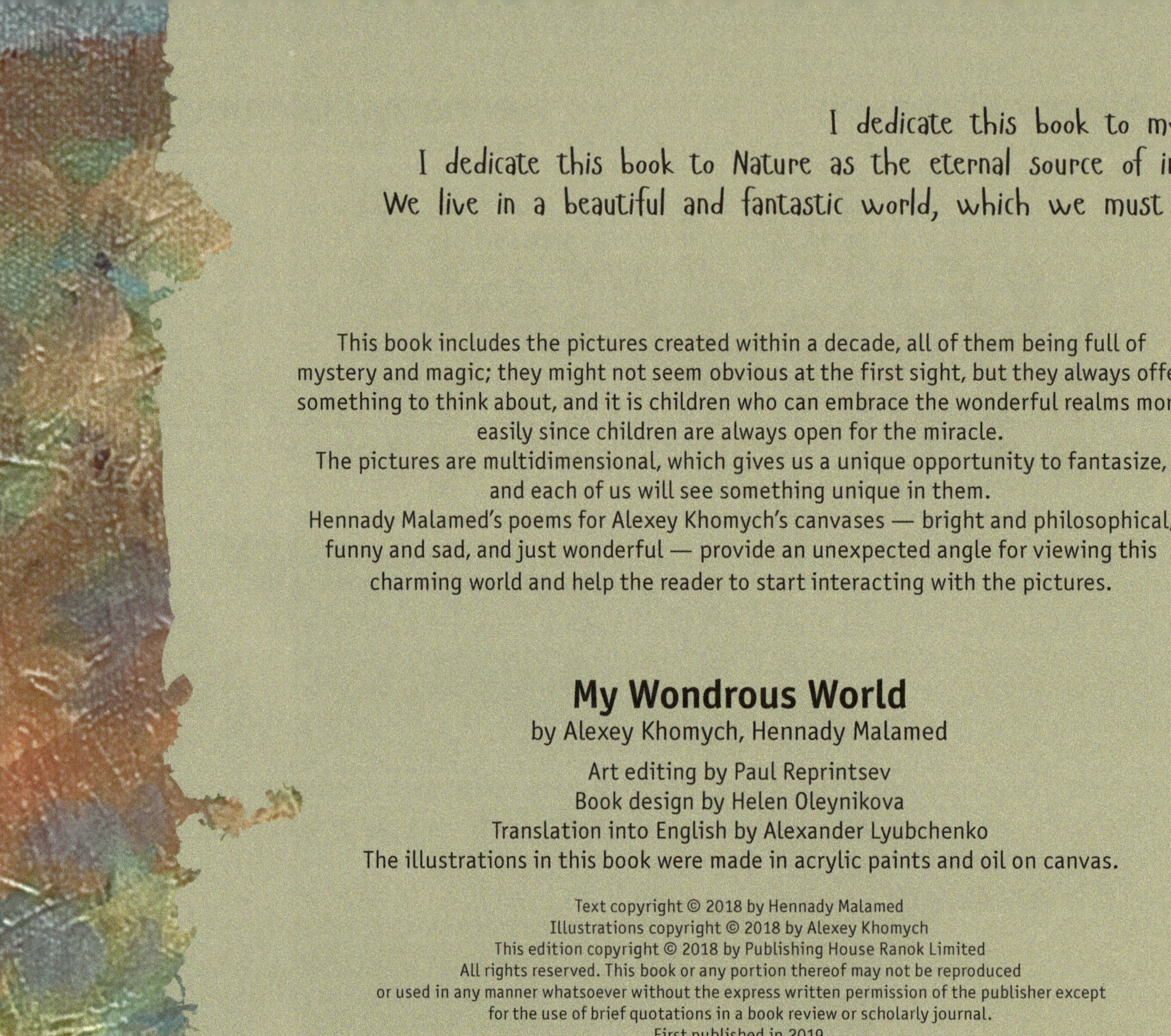

I dedicate this book to my mother.
I dedicate this book to Nature as the eternal source of inspiration.
We live in a beautiful and fantastic world, which we must preserve.
— A. K.

This book includes the pictures created within a decade, all of them being full of mystery and magic; they might not seem obvious at the first sight, but they always offer something to think about, and it is children who can embrace the wonderful realms more easily since children are always open for the miracle.
The pictures are multidimensional, which gives us a unique opportunity to fantasize, and each of us will see something unique in them.
Hennady Malamed's poems for Alexey Khomych's canvases — bright and philosophical, funny and sad, and just wonderful — provide an unexpected angle for viewing this charming world and help the reader to start interacting with the pictures.

My Wondrous World

by Alexey Khomych, Hennady Malamed

Art editing by Paul Reprintsev
Book design by Helen Oleynikova
Translation into English by Alexander Lyubchenko
The illustrations in this book were made in acrylic paints and oil on canvas.

Text copyright © 2018 by Hennady Malamed
Illustrations copyright © 2018 by Alexey Khomych
This edition copyright © 2018 by Publishing House Ranok Limited
All rights reserved. This book or any portion thereof may not be reproduced
or used in any manner whatsoever without the express written permission of the publisher except
for the use of brief quotations in a book review or scholarly journal.
First published in 2019
ISBN 978-617-09-5169-4
Publishing House Ranok Limited
135-27 Kibalchicha street, Kharkiv, Ukraine, 61071
MAGE is a division of Publishing House Ranok Limited
For more information, contact MAGE,
21a Kosmichna street., Entrance 1, Floor 8,
Kharkiv, Ukraine, 61145

Email: booksmage@gmail.com
Editor page: fb.me/MAGEhut

My Wondrous World

Illustrations by **Alexey Khomych**
Written by **Hennady Malamed**

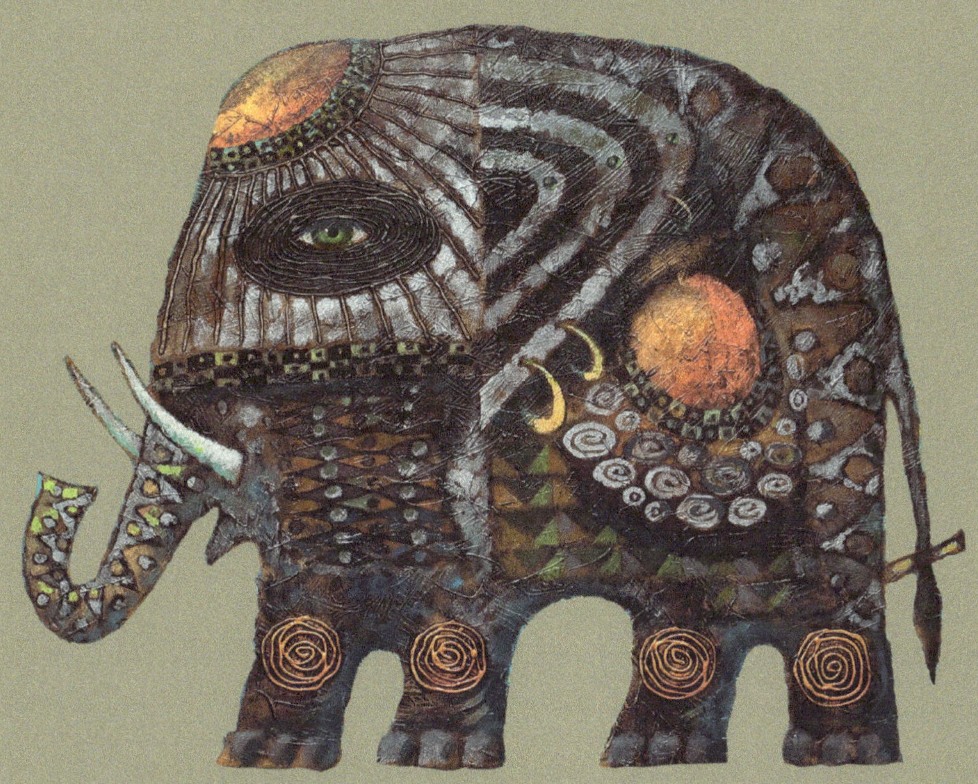

Rhymed Paintings and Painted Rhymes

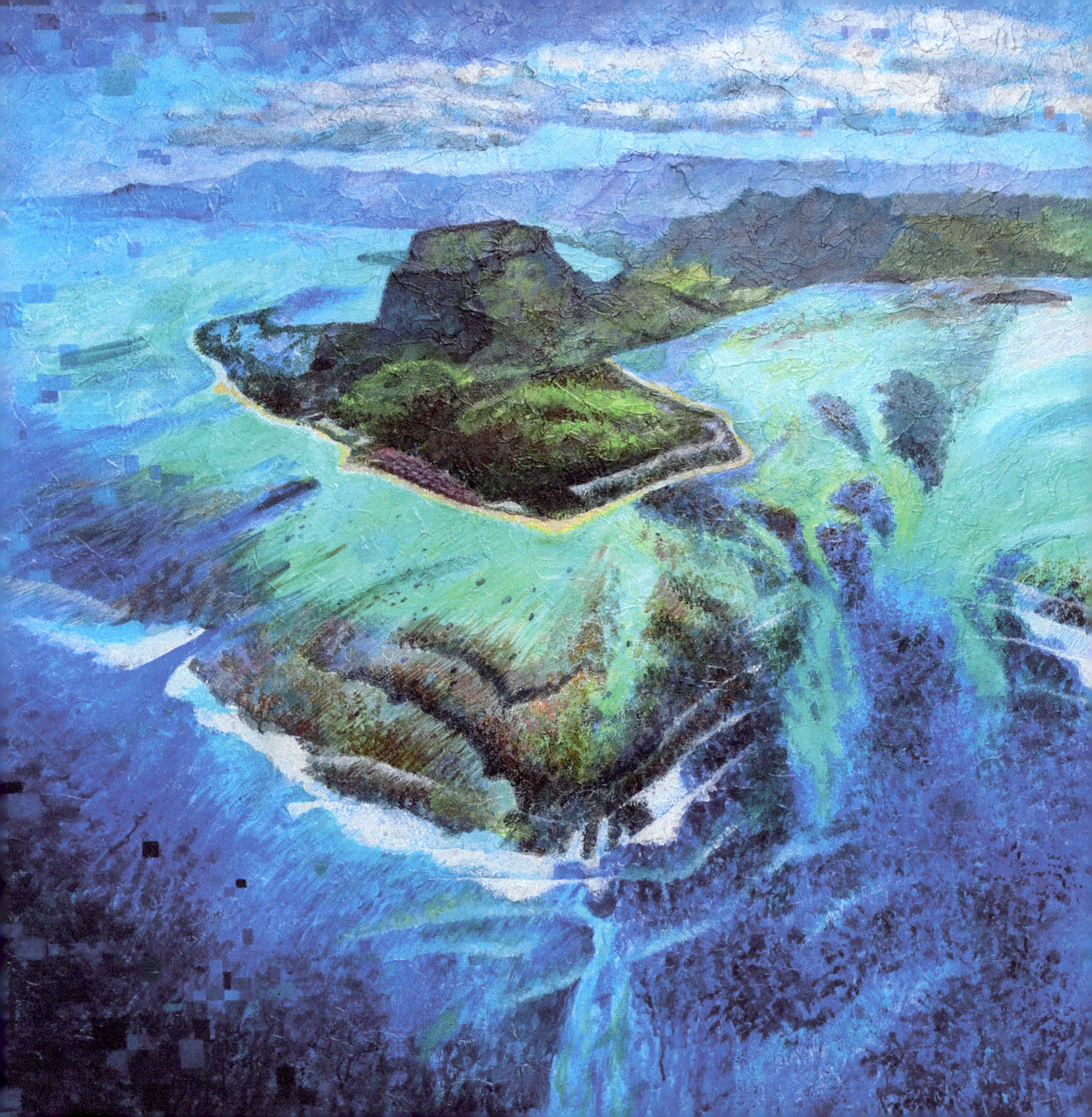

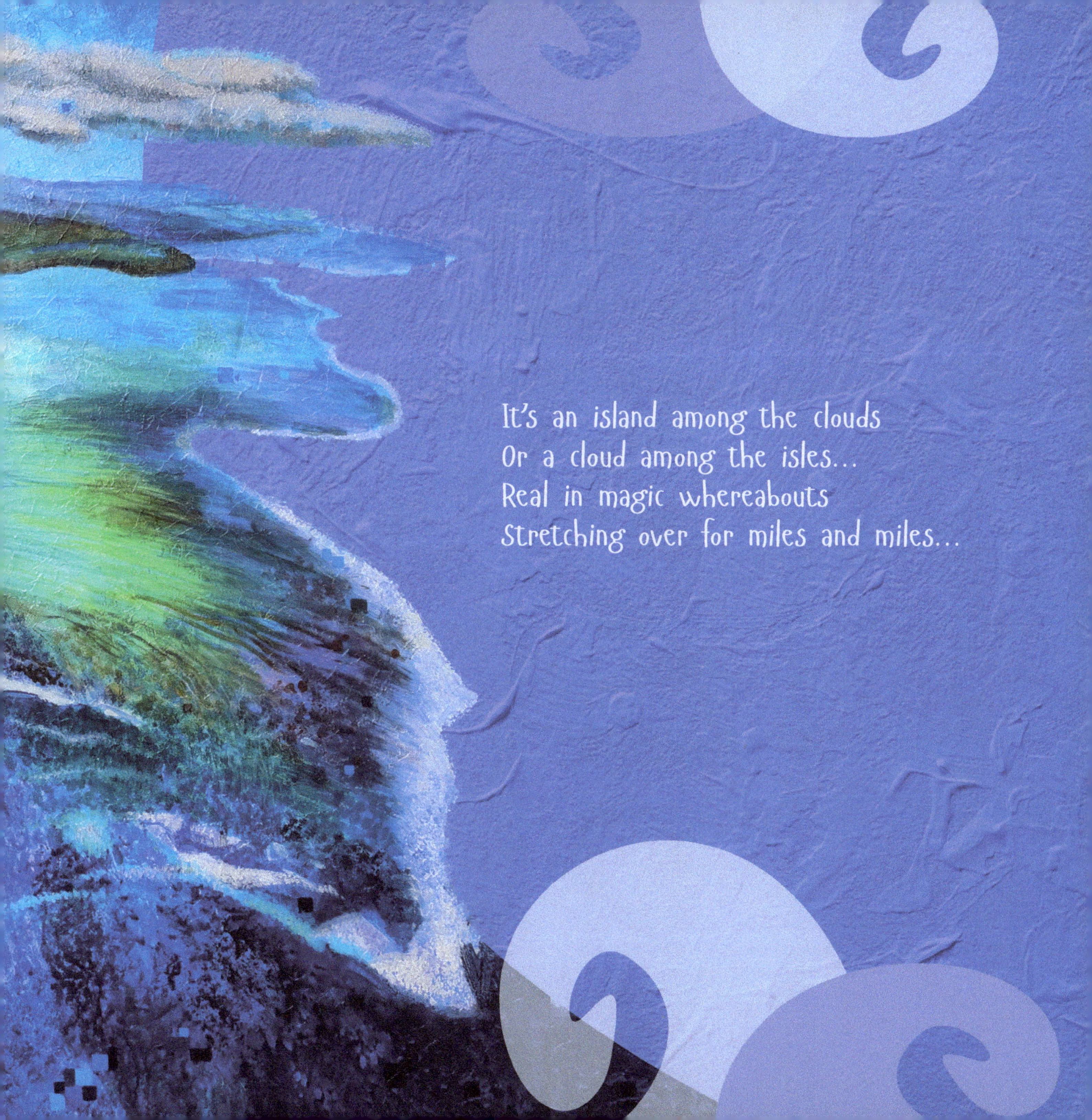
It's an island among the clouds
Or a cloud among the isles...
Real in magic whereabouts
Stretching over for miles and miles...

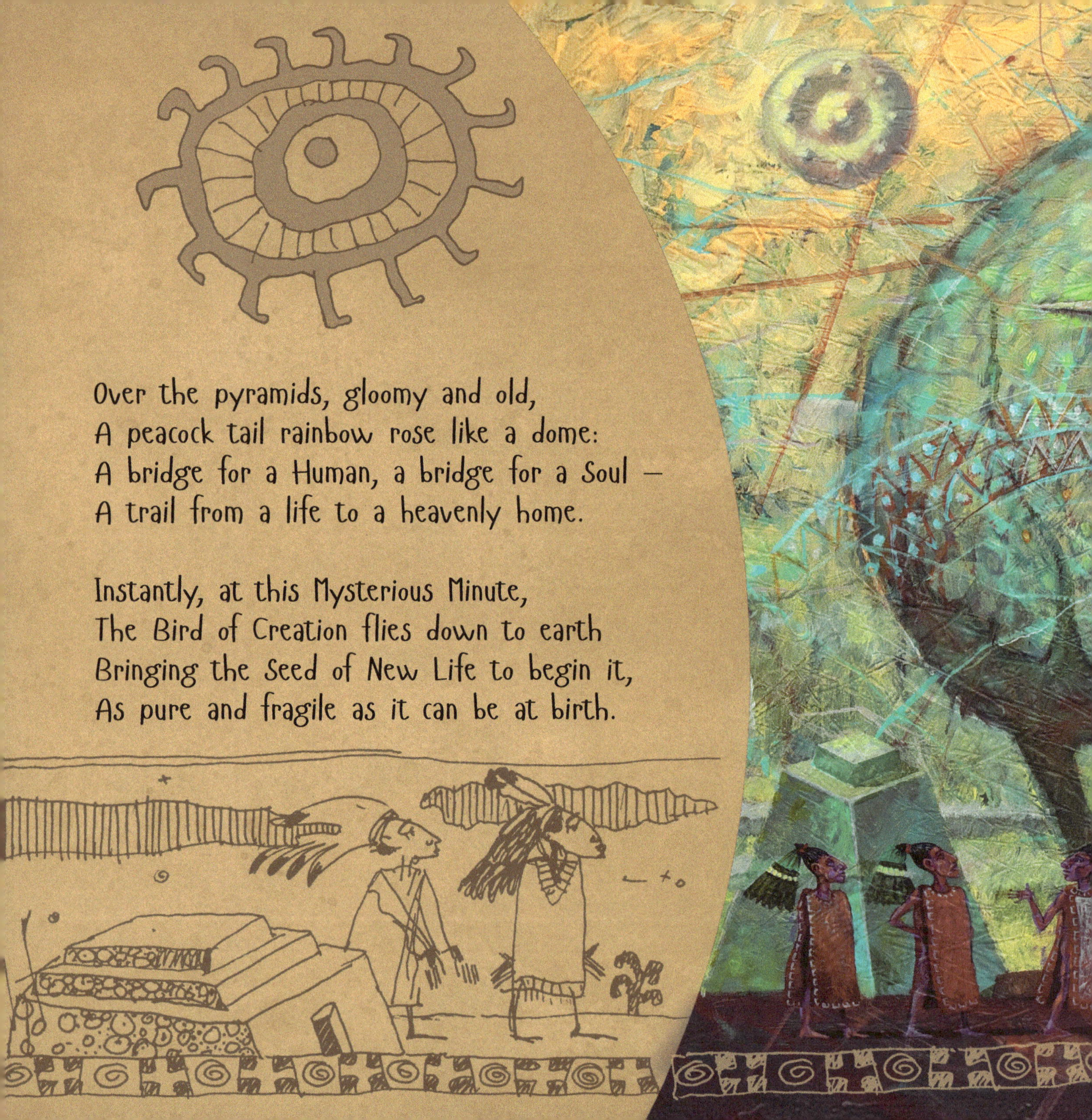

Over the pyramids, gloomy and old,
A peacock tail rainbow rose like a dome:
A bridge for a Human, a bridge for a Soul —
A trail from a life to a heavenly home.

Instantly, at this Mysterious Minute,
The Bird of Creation flies down to earth
Bringing the Seed of New Life to begin it,
As pure and fragile as it can be at birth.

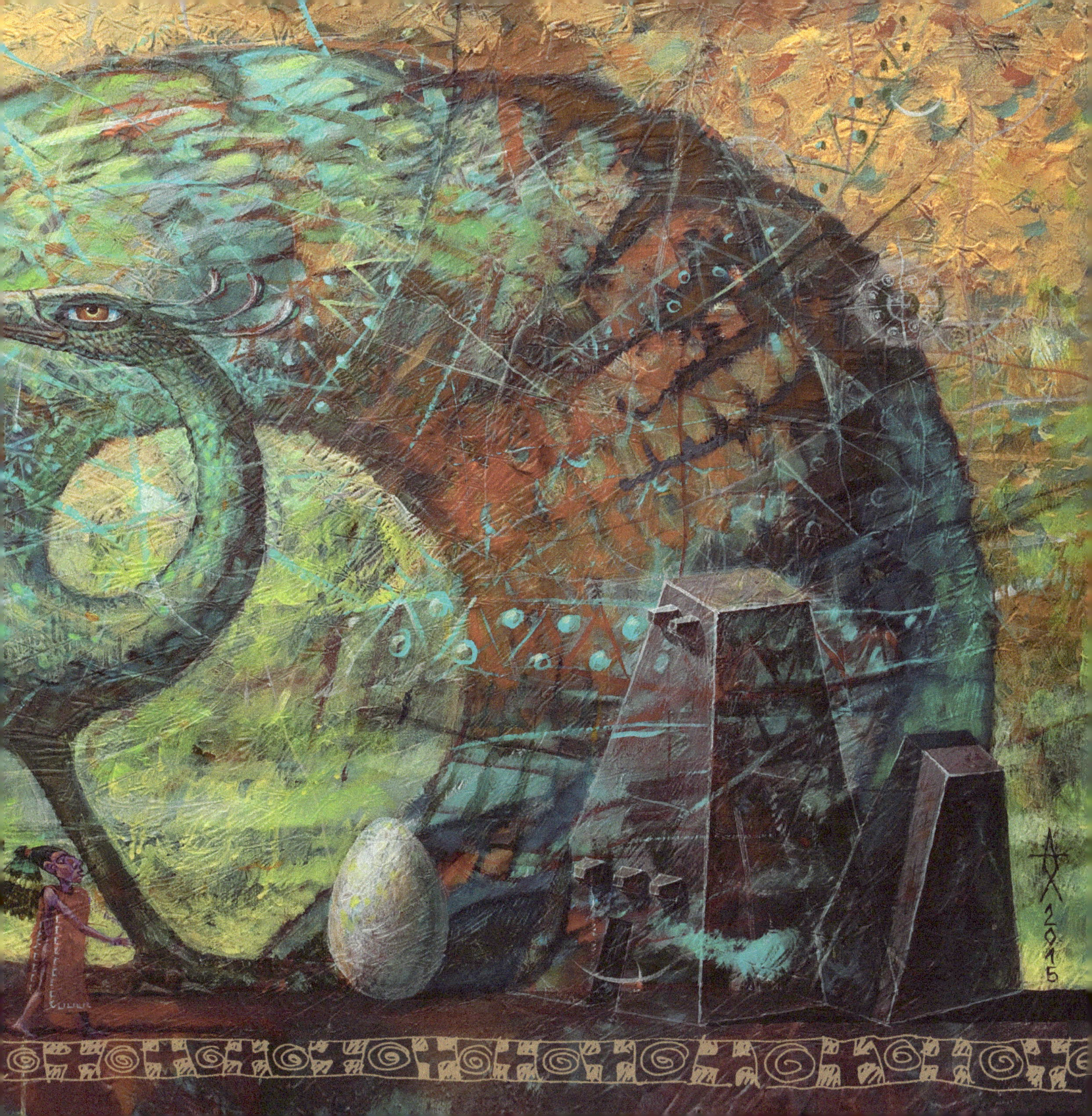

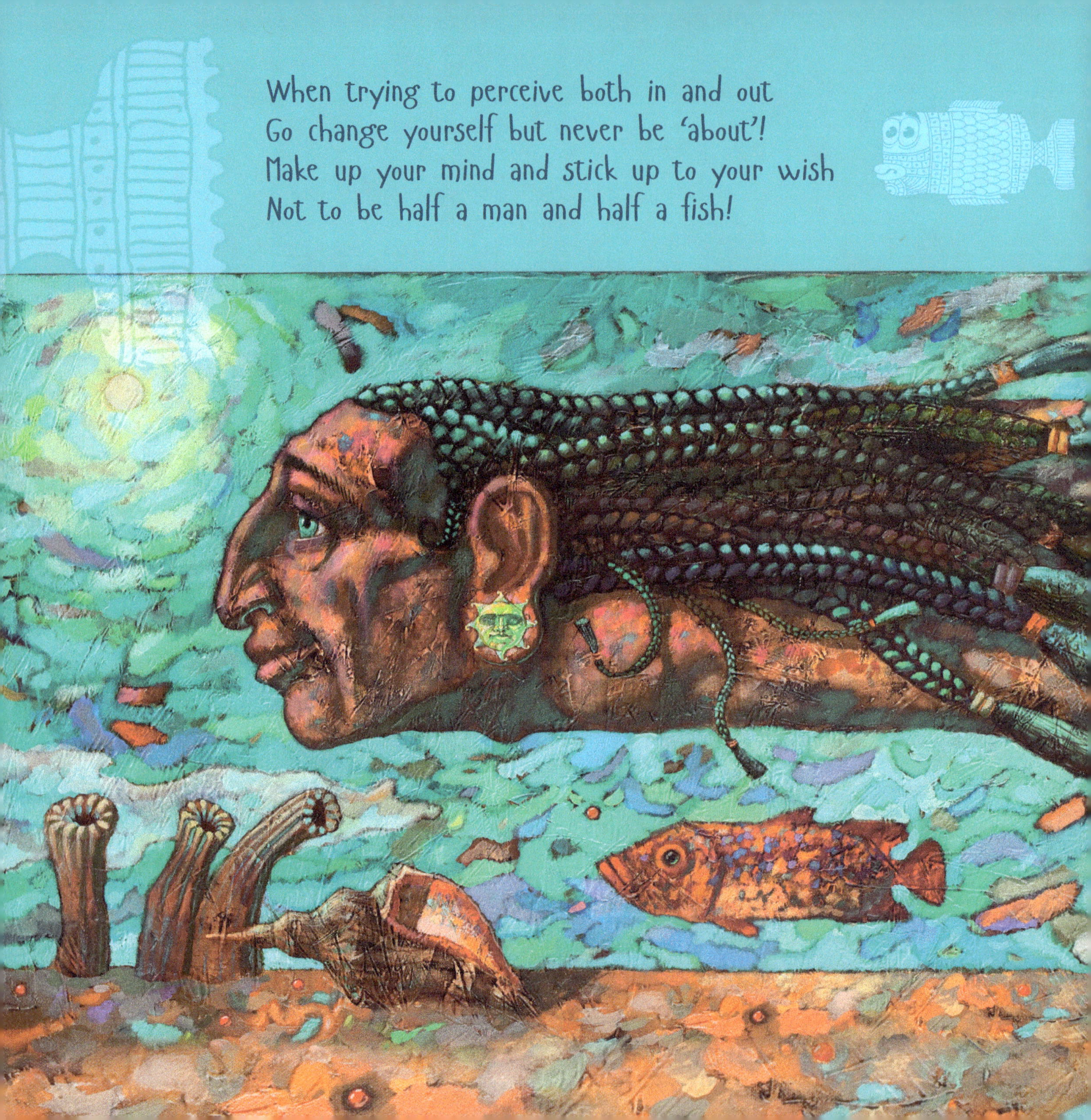

When trying to perceive both in and out
Go change yourself but never be 'about'!
Make up your mind and stick up to your wish
Not to be half a man and half a fish!

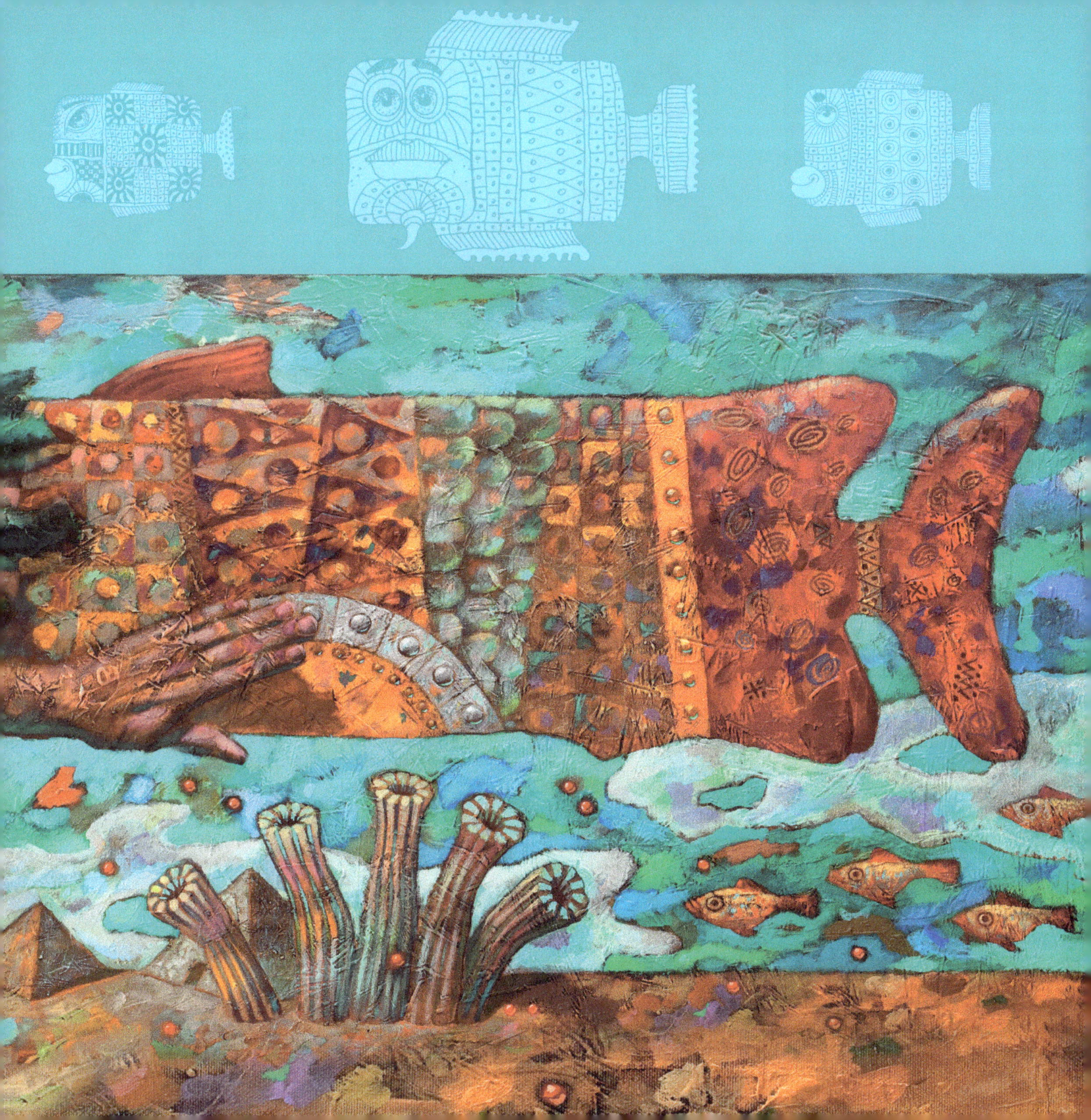

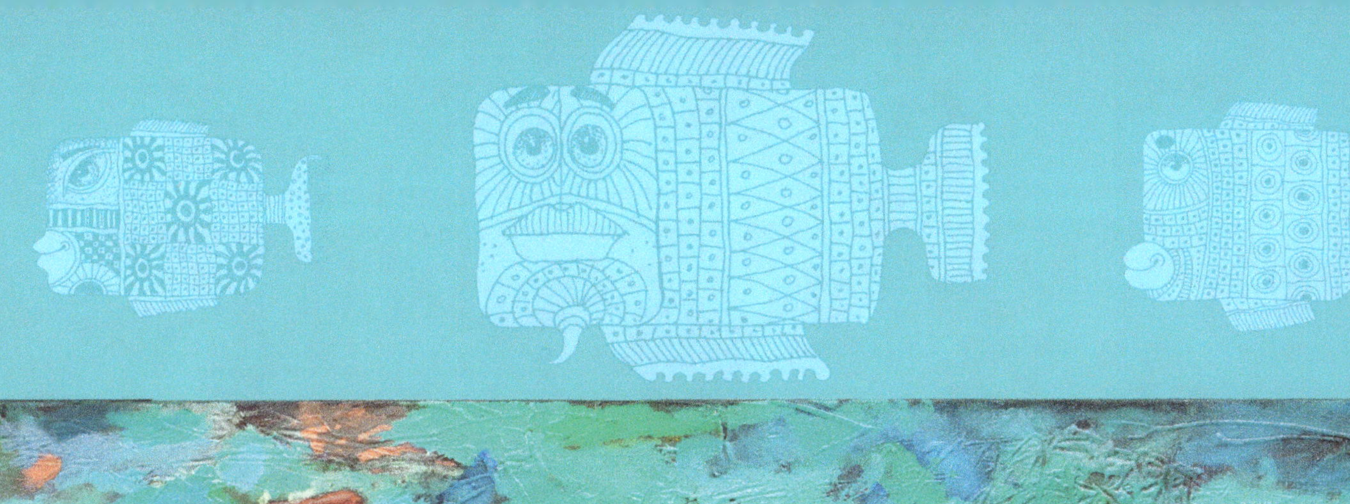

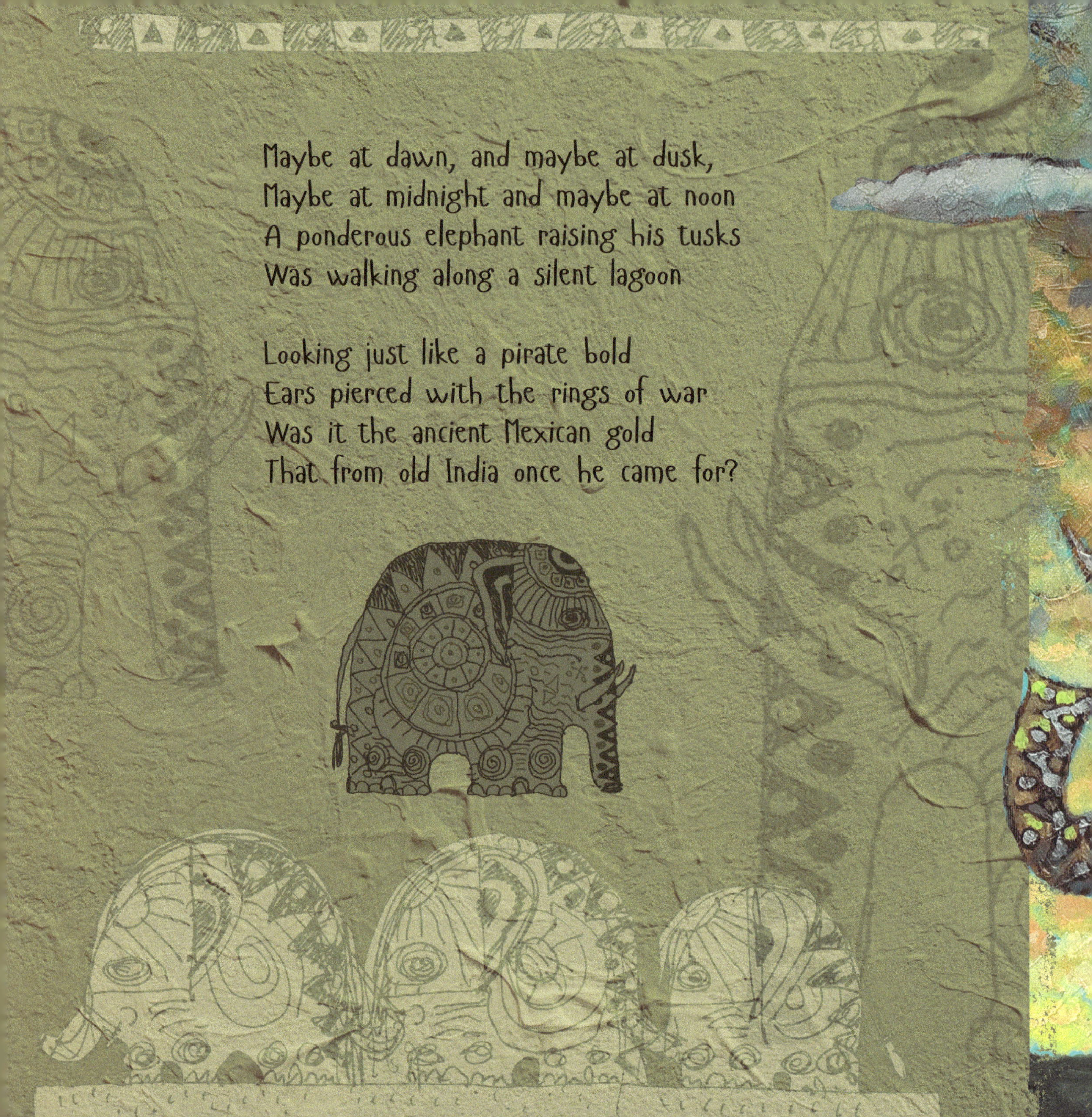

Maybe at dawn, and maybe at dusk,
Maybe at midnight and maybe at noon
A ponderous elephant raising his tusks
Was walking along a silent lagoon

Looking just like a pirate bold
Ears pierced with the rings of war
Was it the ancient Mexican gold
That from old India once he came for?

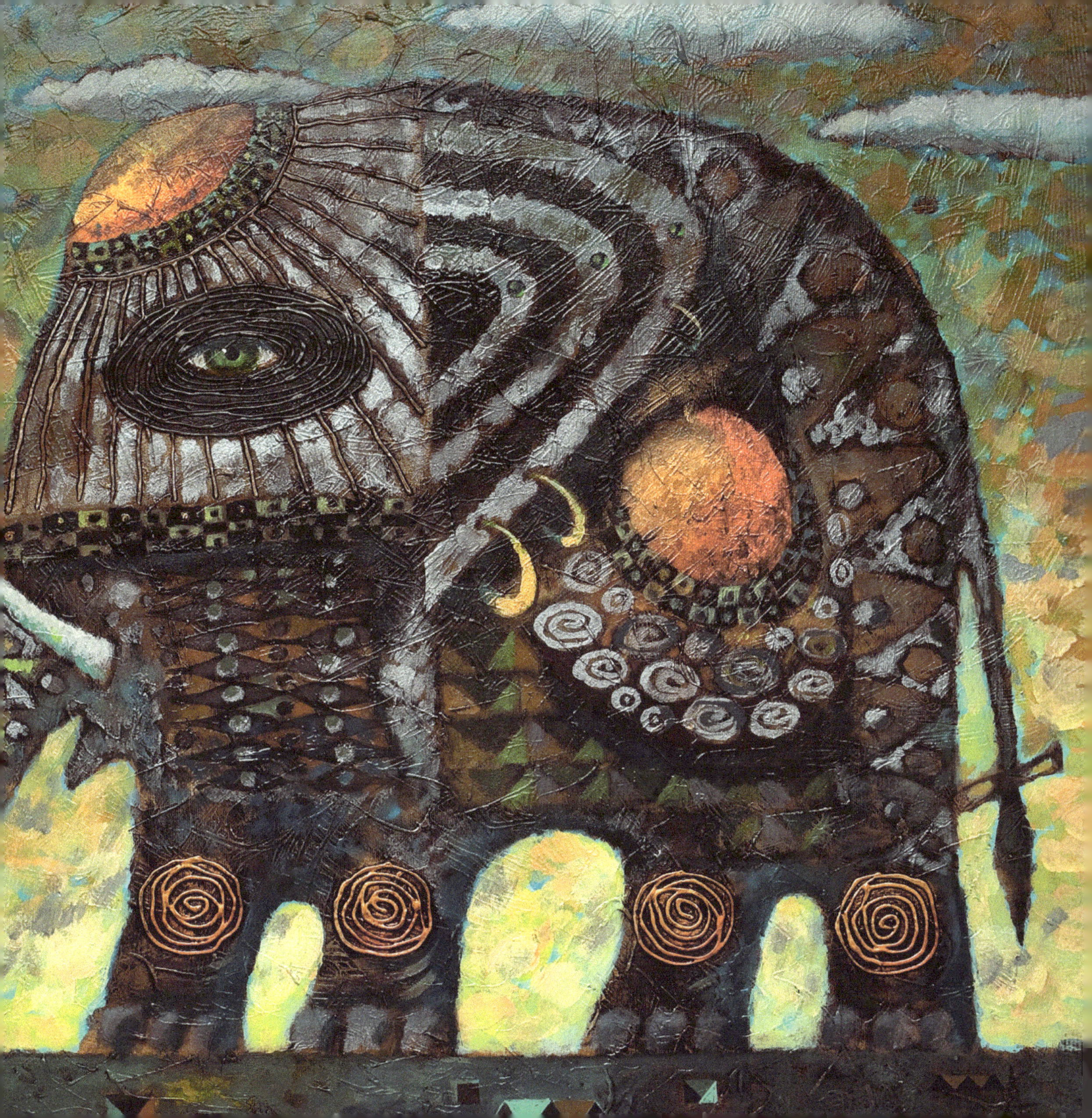

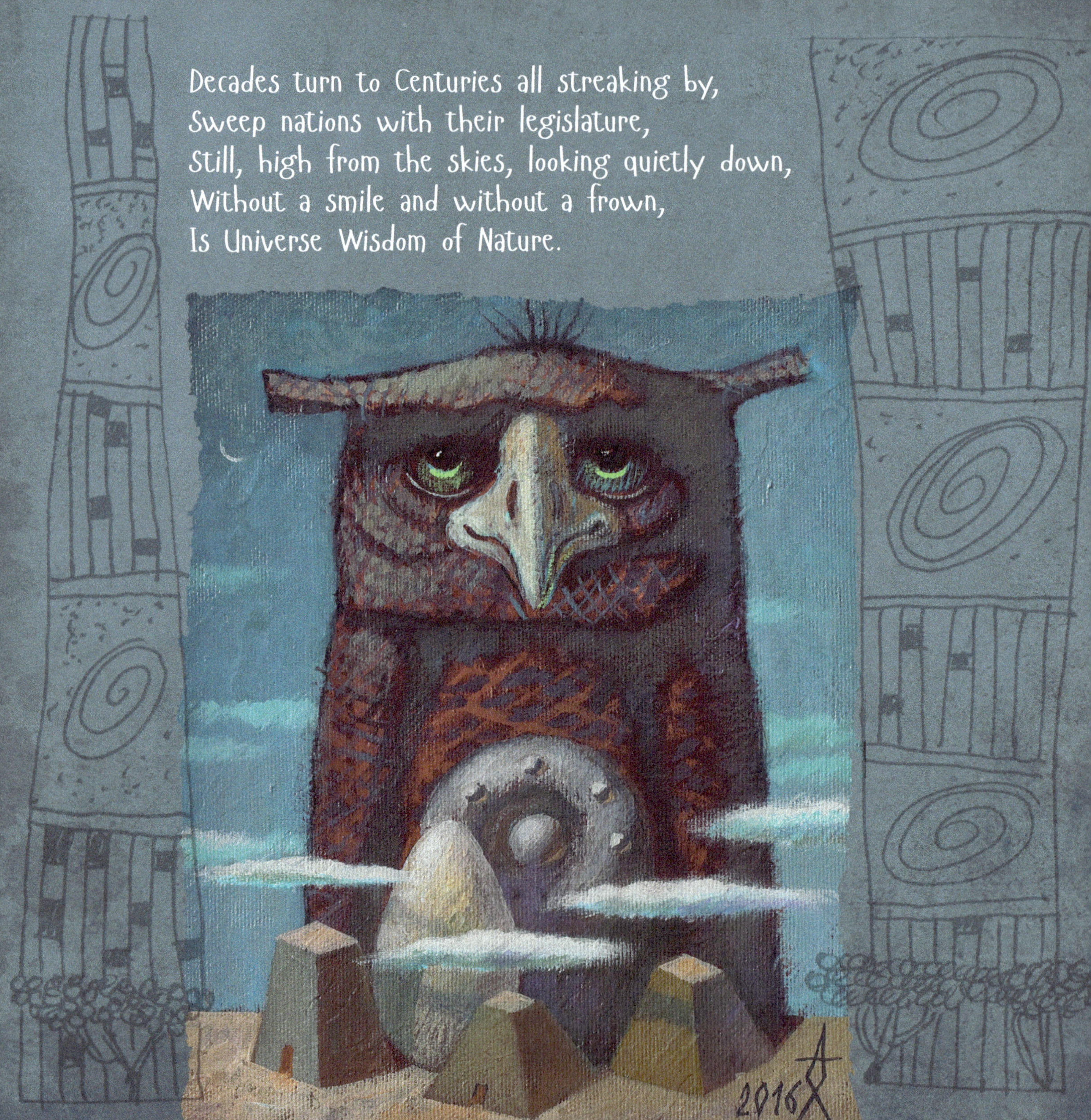

Decades turn to Centuries all streaking by,
Sweep nations with their legislature,
Still, high from the skies, looking quietly down,
Without a smile and without a frown,
Is Universe Wisdom of Nature.

2016

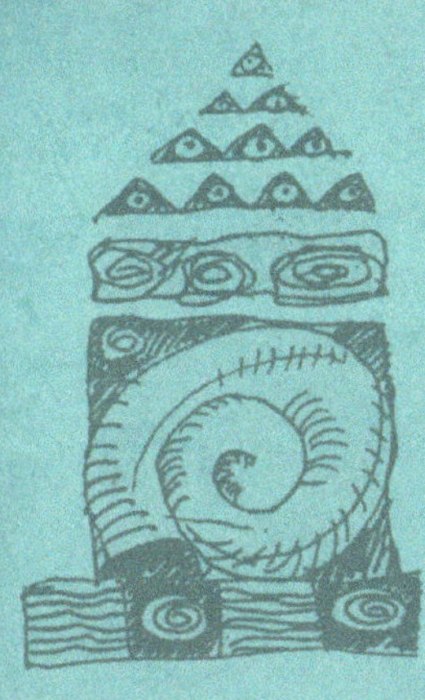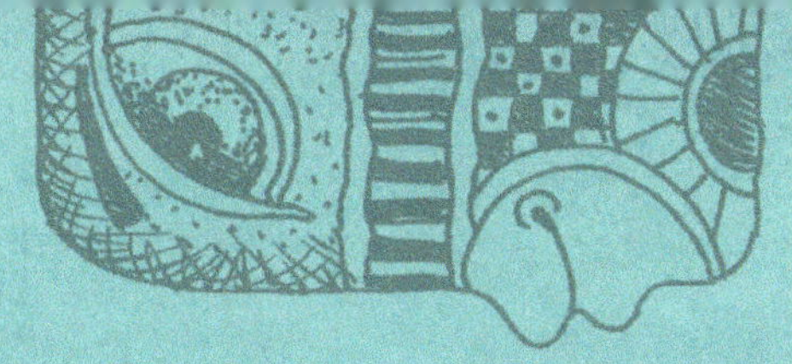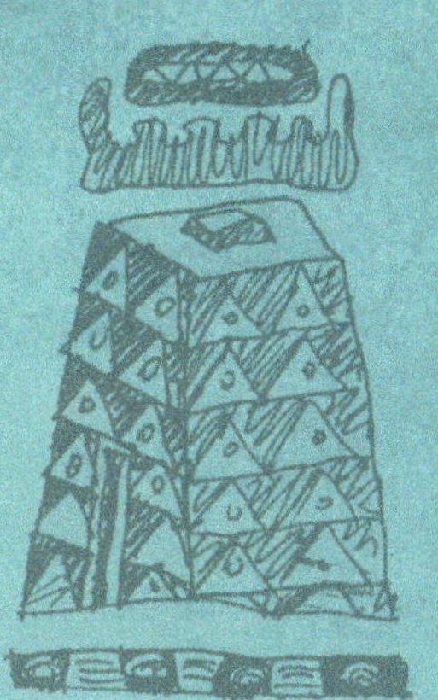

To catch the Fortune by its lip or tail
Does not exactly mean you are its master,
As Fortune may transform into Disaster,
Who knows — which of those will win or fail?

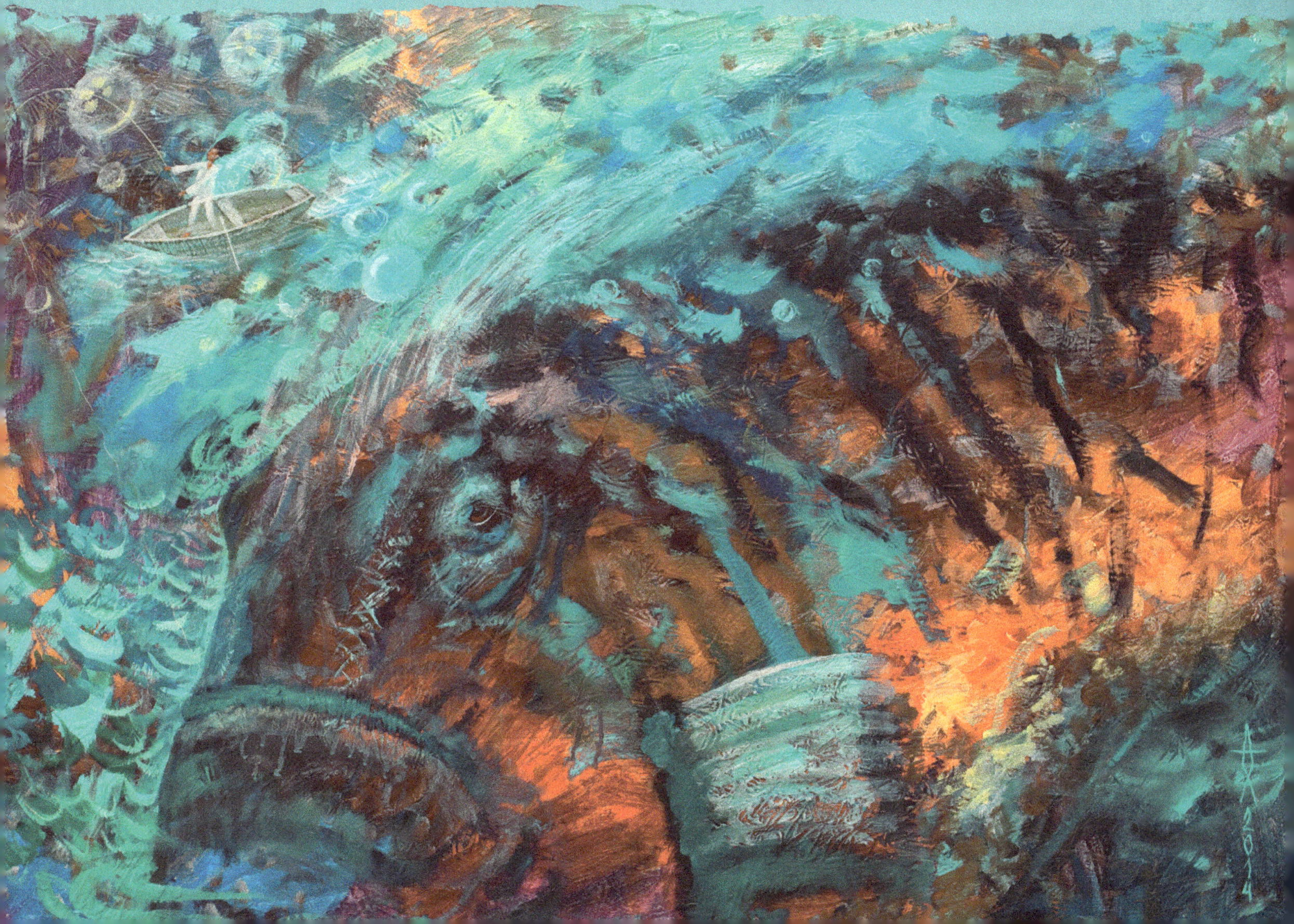

A newt, one of freshwater guys
Arrived in ocean bold and strong
To get the local folk surprised
With ultra-fashionable disguise,
And not to let it all go wrong!

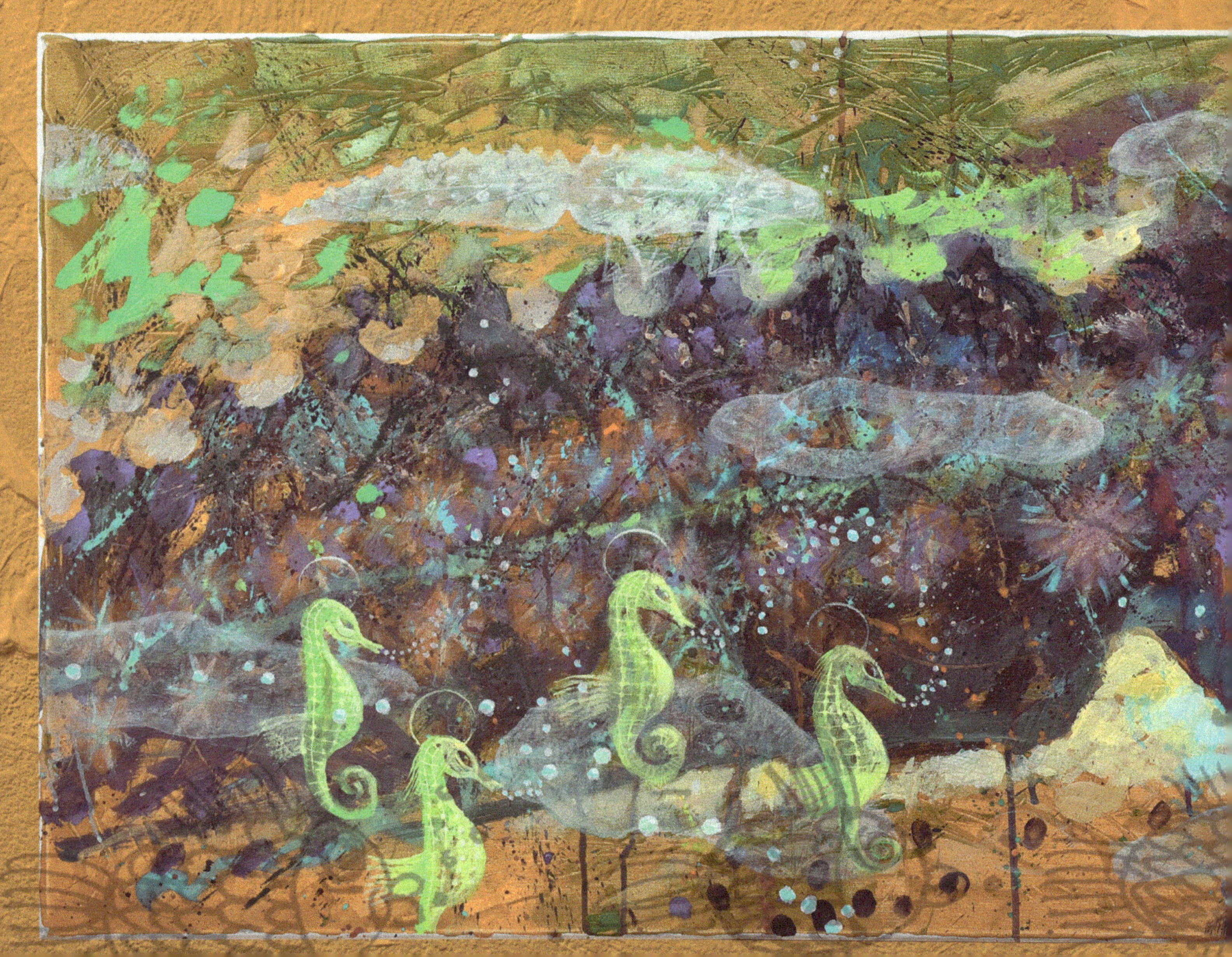

Seahorses following him gaily
And jellyfish like clouds around,
And Him — parading and unfailing,
Just like a favorite prevailing
And looking down on everyone.

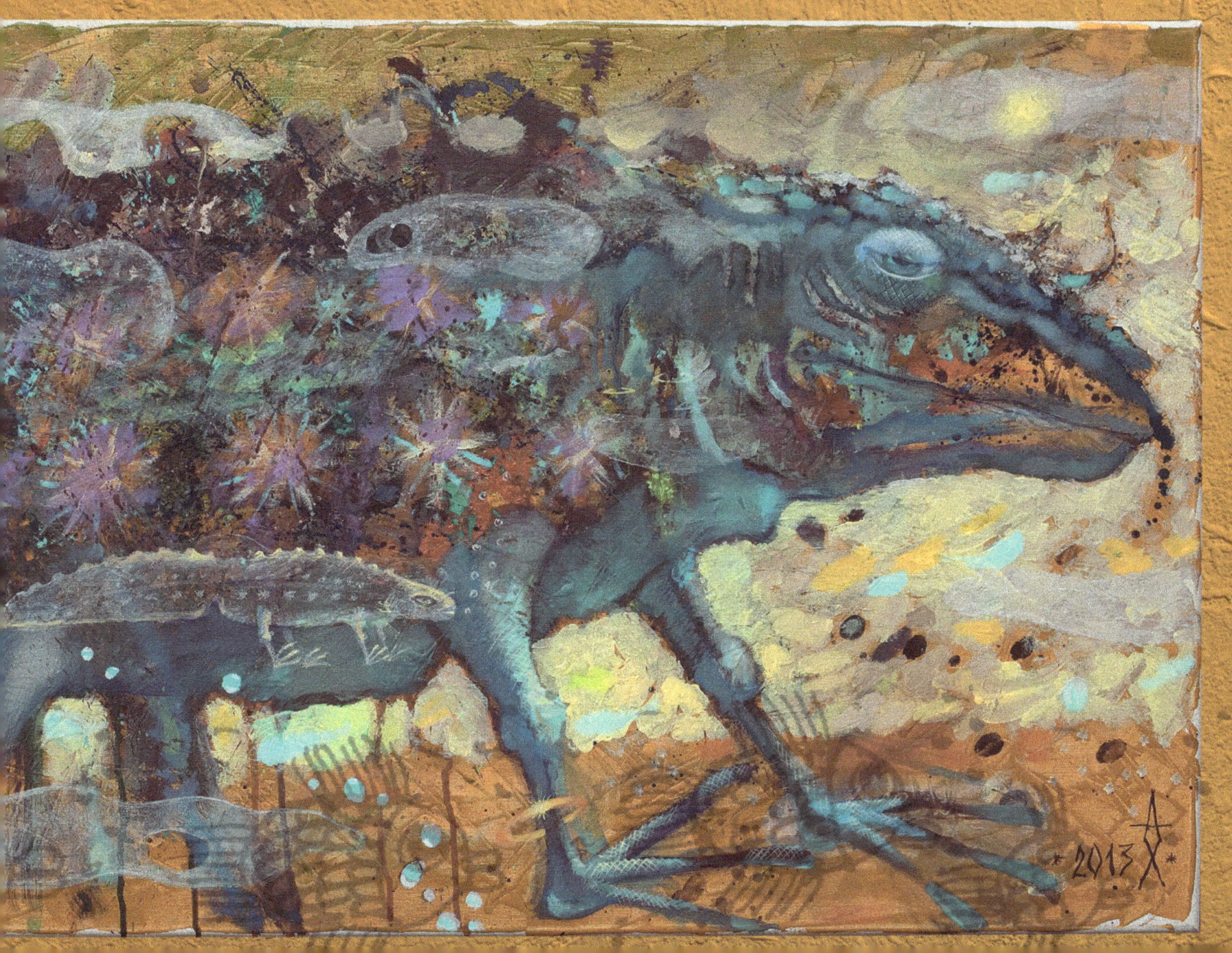

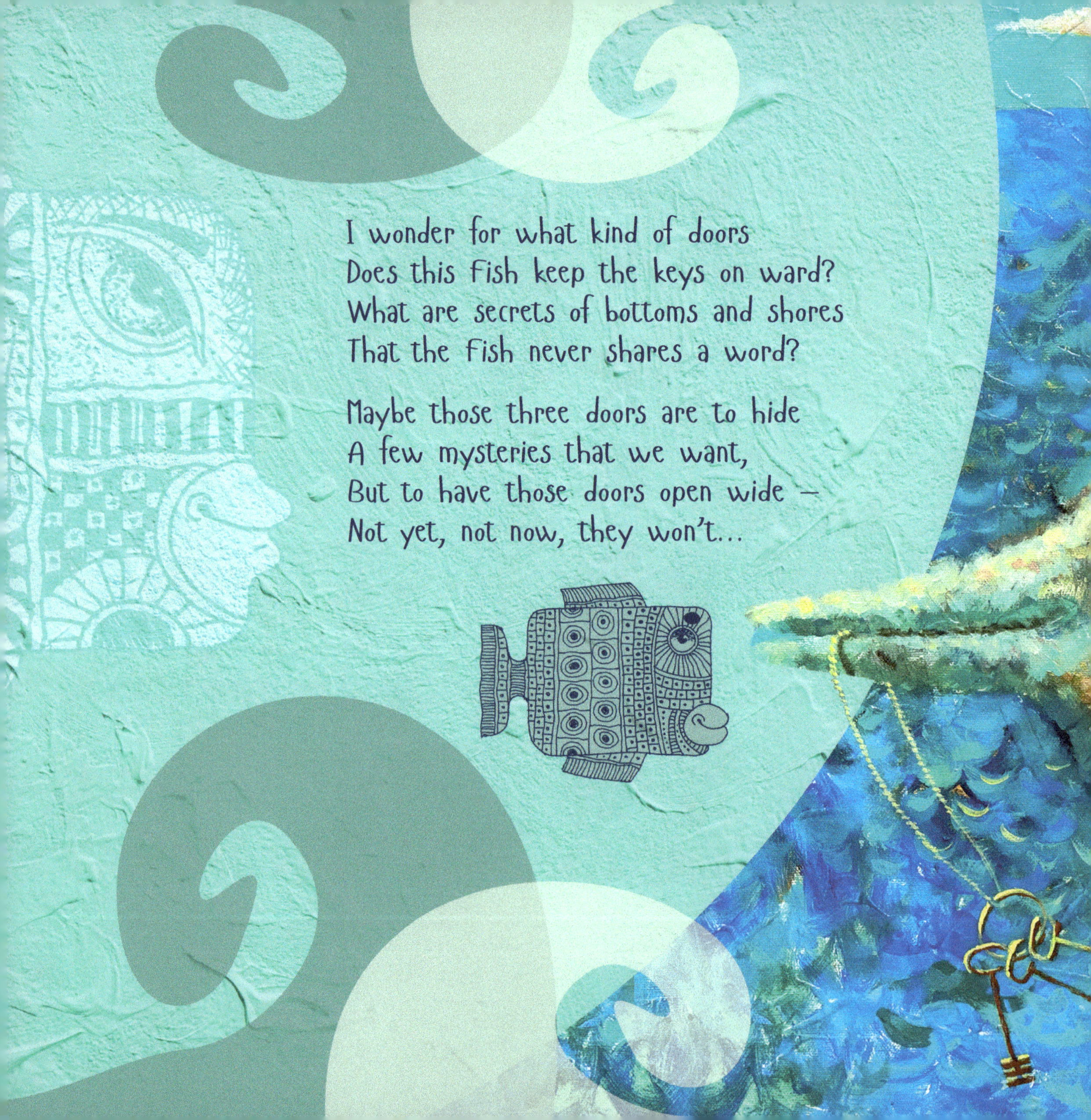

I wonder for what kind of doors
Does this fish keep the keys on ward?
What are secrets of bottoms and shores
That the fish never shares a word?

Maybe those three doors are to hide
A few mysteries that we want,
But to have those doors open wide —
Not yet, not now, they won't…

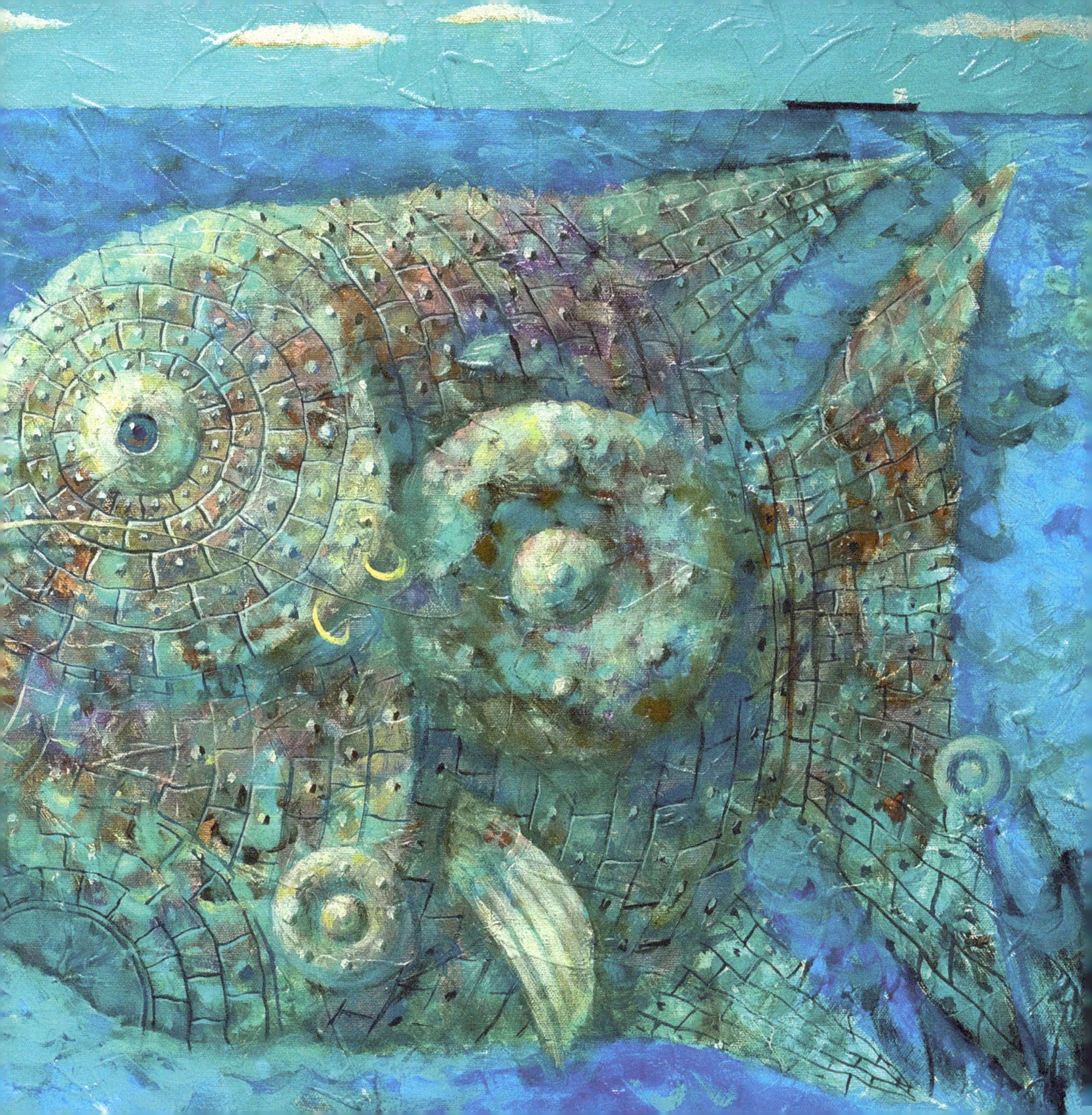

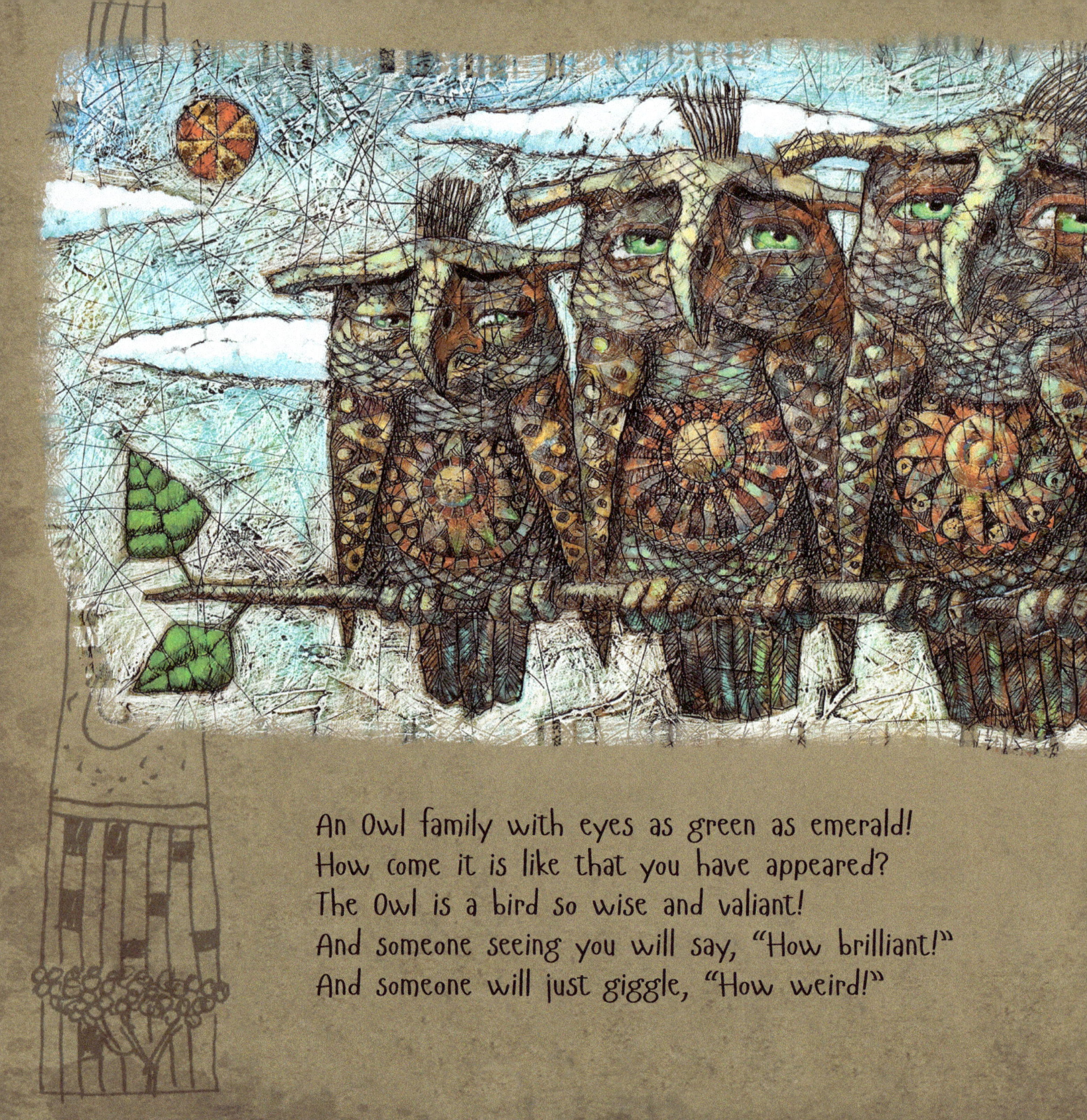

An Owl family with eyes as green as emerald!
How come it is like that you have appeared?
The Owl is a bird so wise and valiant!
And someone seeing you will say, "How brilliant!"
And someone will just giggle, "How weird!"

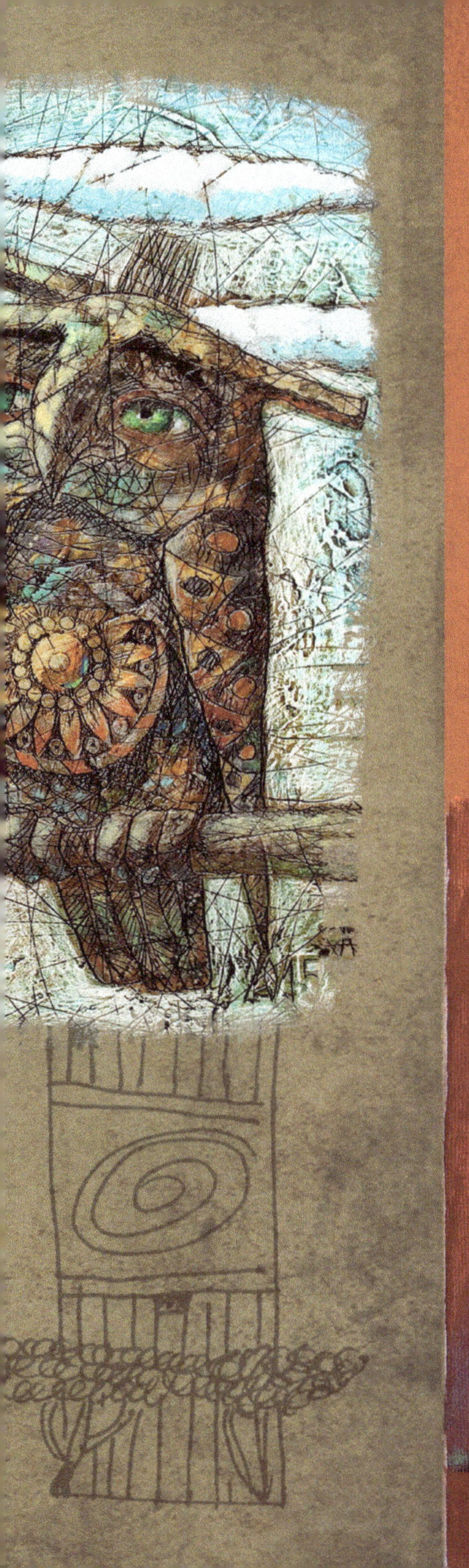

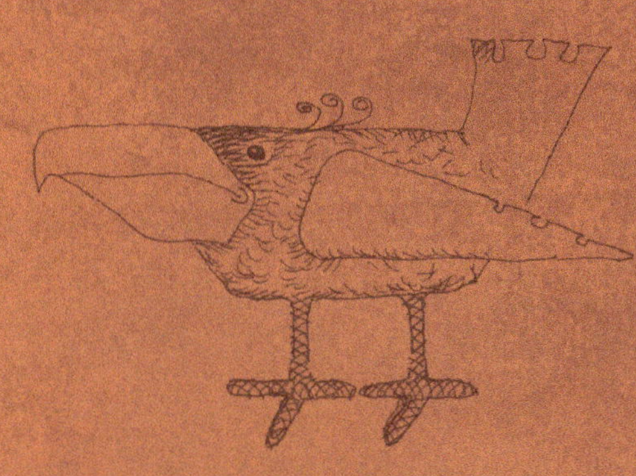

The Crows expect in their batch
An unusual chick to hatch —
A mighty Genius full of wisdom,
Doing everything from scratch.
And the raffle is beginning:
What if there is a Genie?

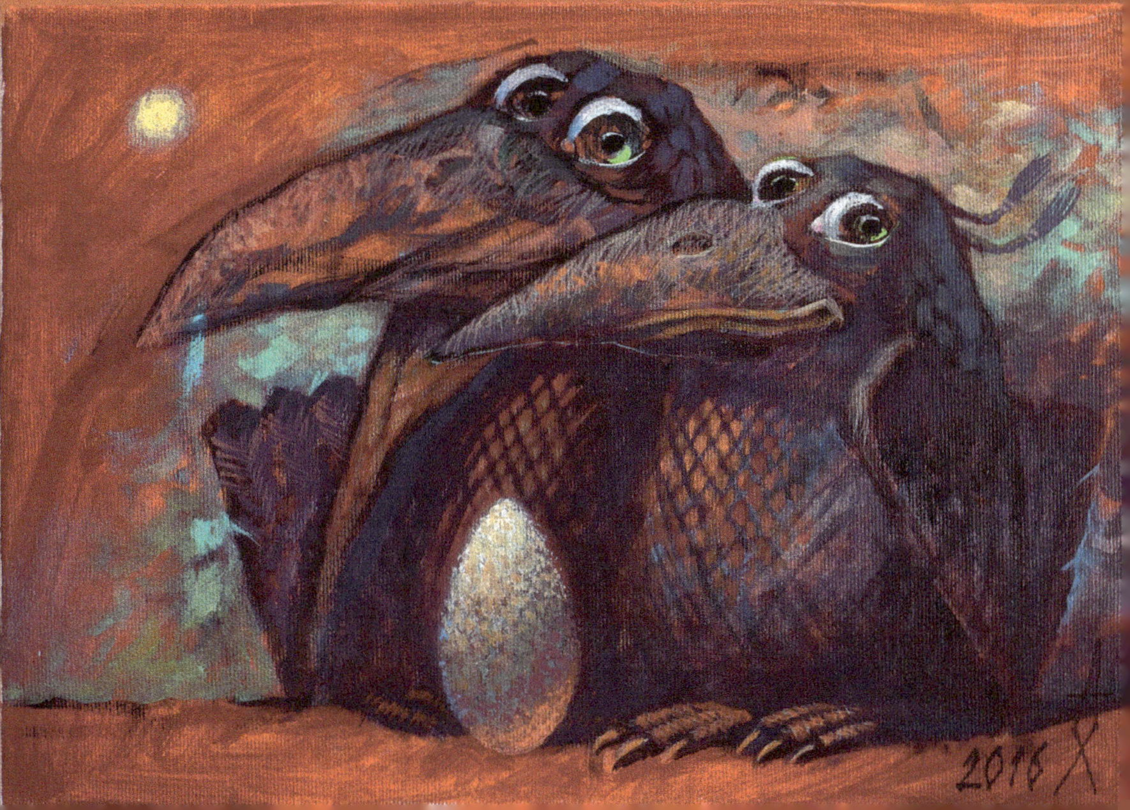

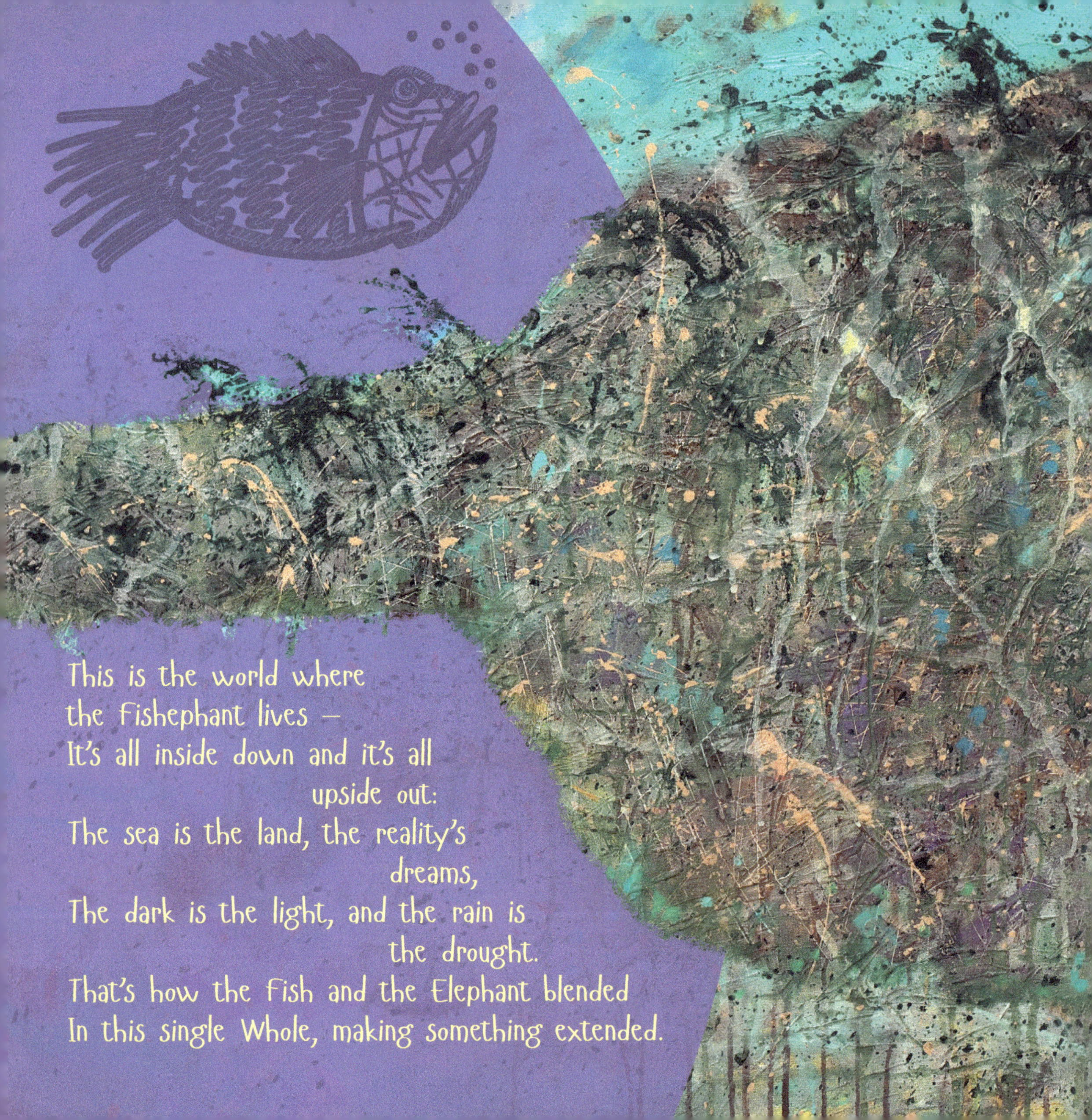

This is the world where
the Fishephant lives —
It's all inside down and it's all
                          upside out:
The sea is the land, the reality's
                          dreams,
The dark is the light, and the rain is
                          the drought.
That's how the Fish and the Elephant blended
In this single Whole, making something extended.

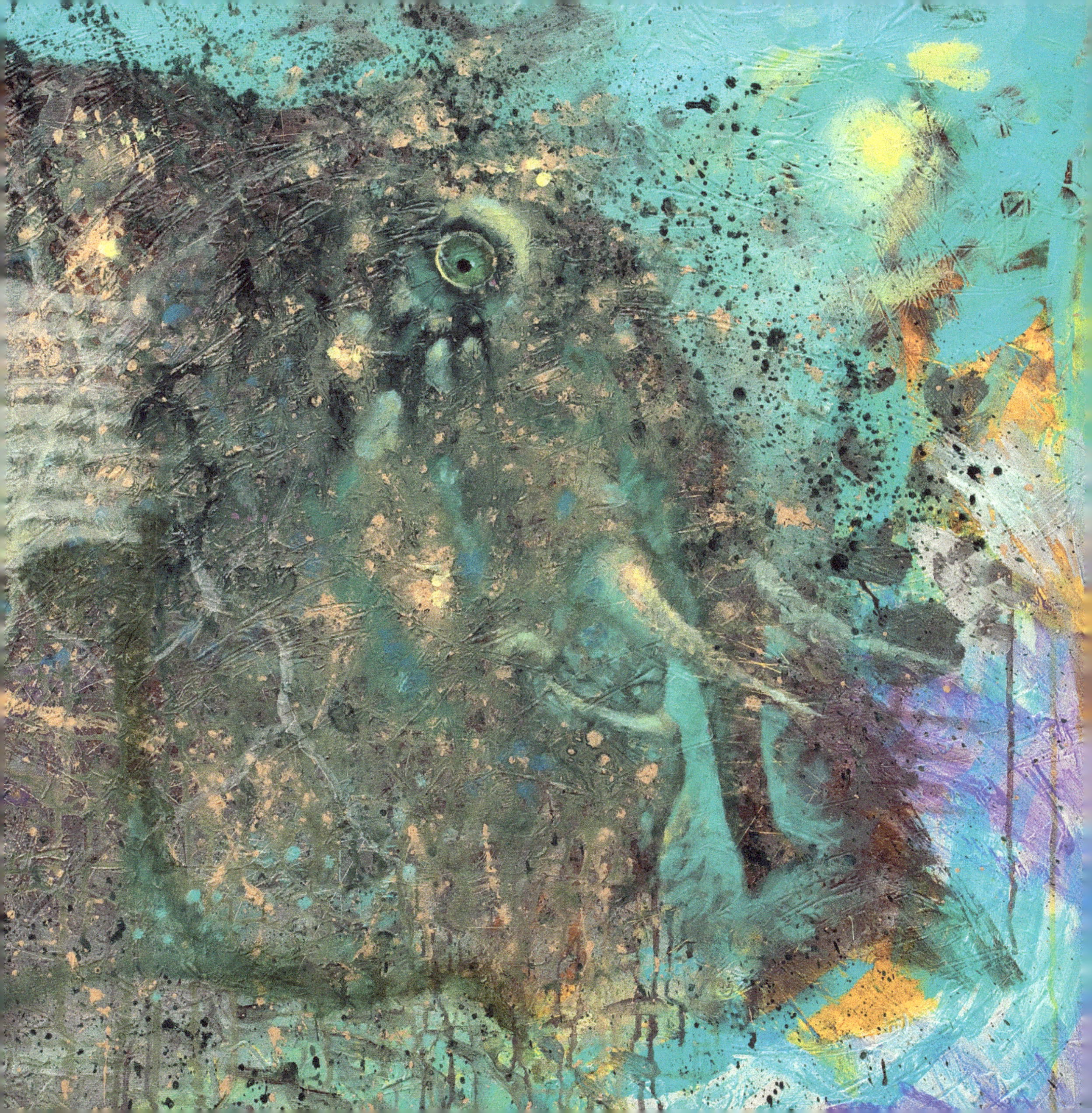

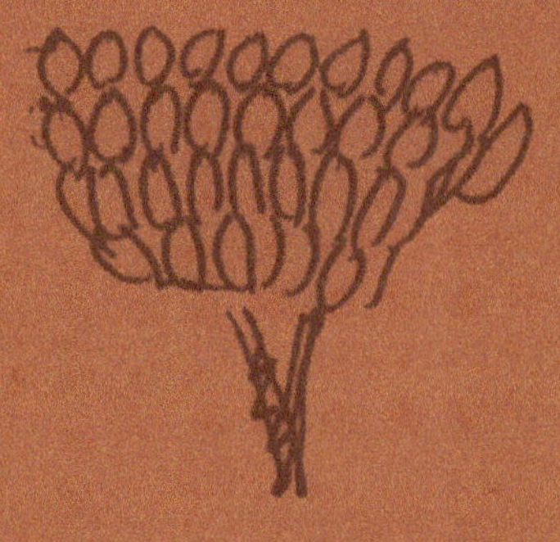

Obstinate, tough, in the wonderful order,
The Camels were wandering forth,
Reaching the edge, and the end, and the border,
Yet, there are no those on the Earth!...

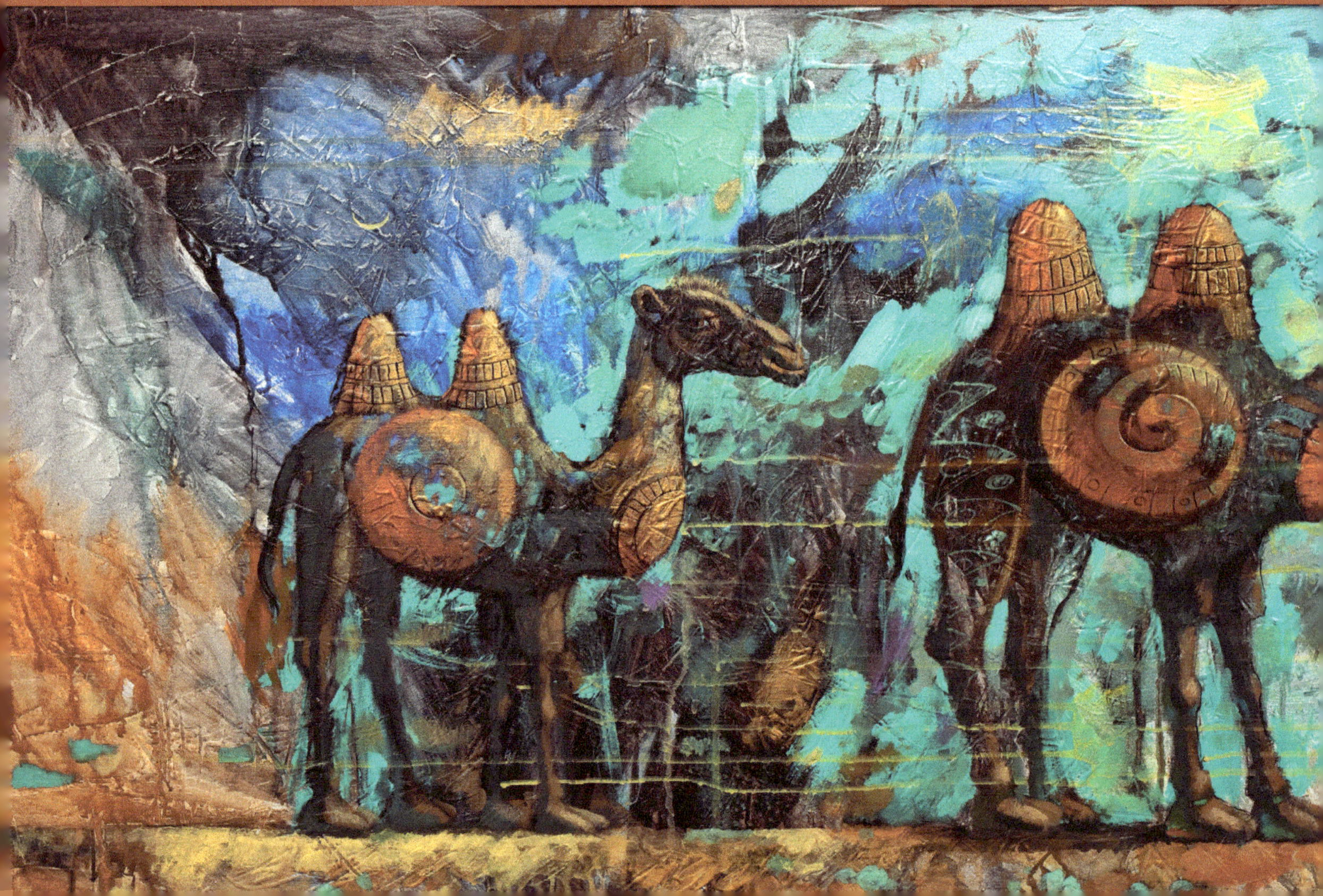

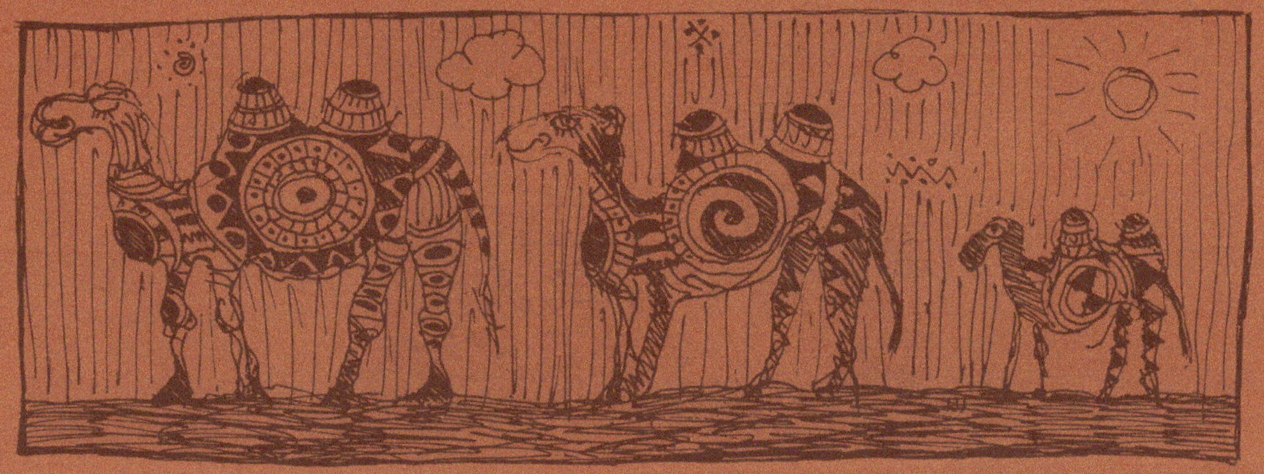

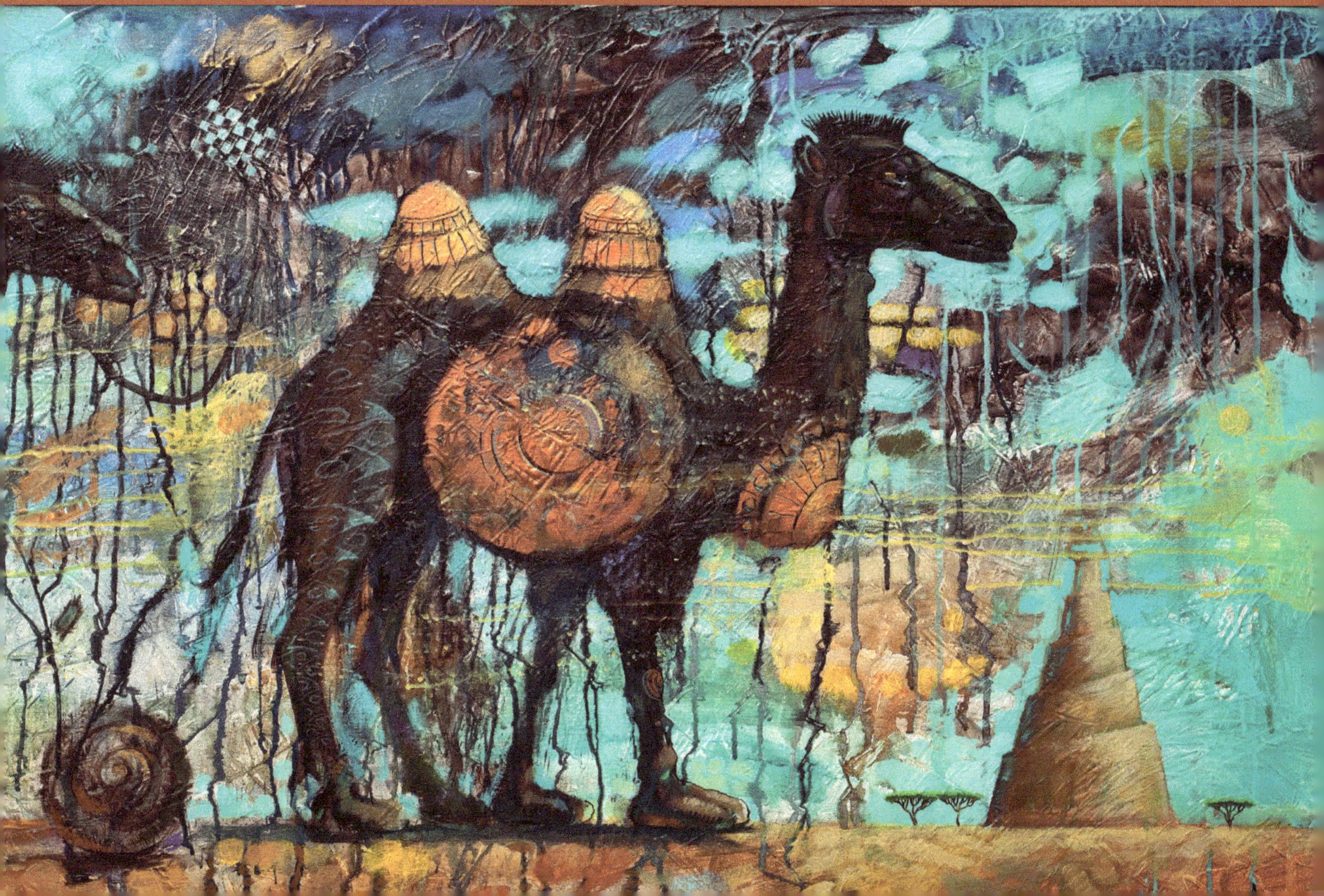

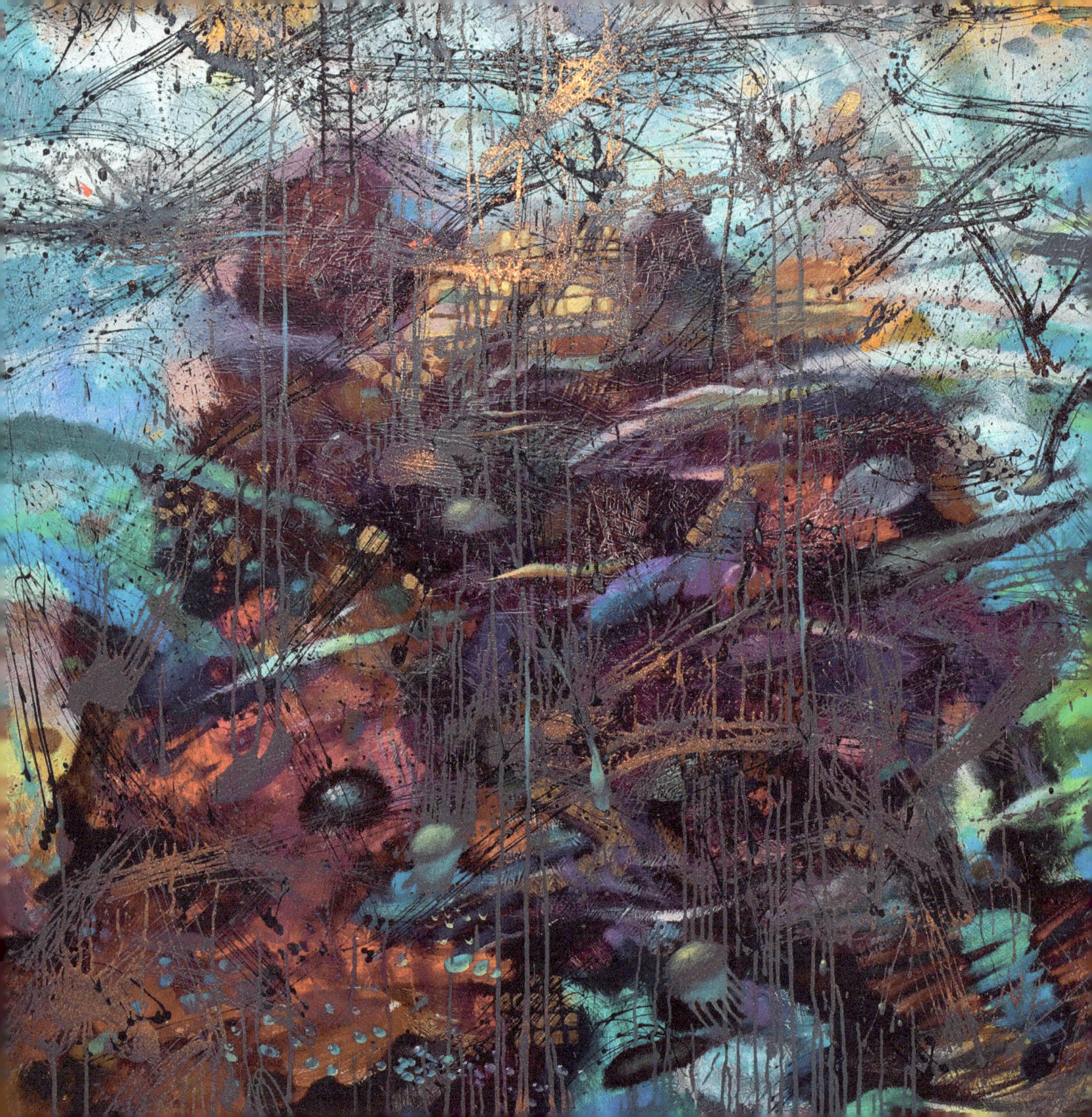

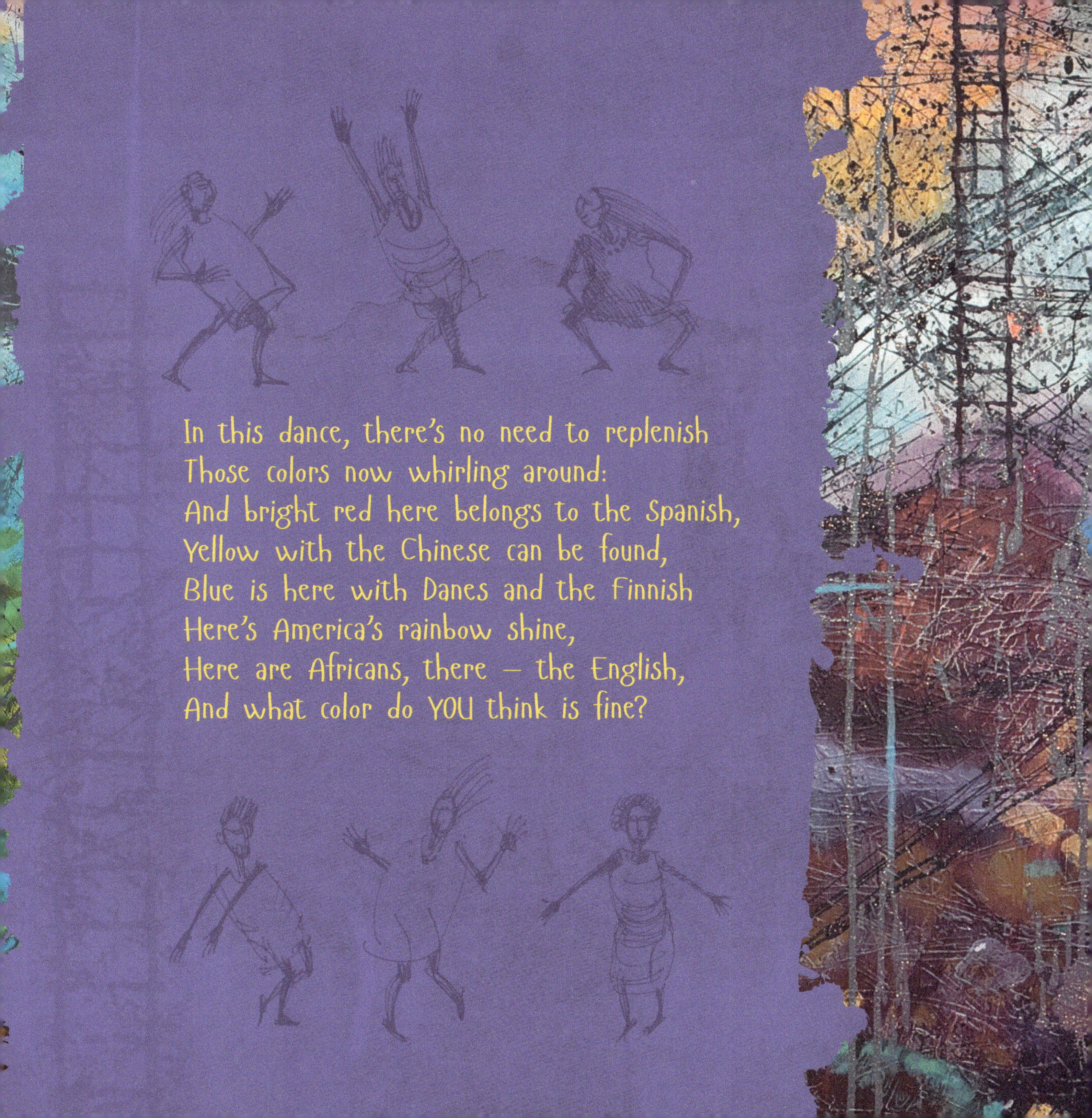

In this dance, there's no need to replenish
Those colors now whirling around:
And bright red here belongs to the Spanish,
Yellow with the Chinese can be found,
Blue is here with Danes and the Finnish
Here's America's rainbow shine,
Here are Africans, there — the English,
And what color do YOU think is fine?

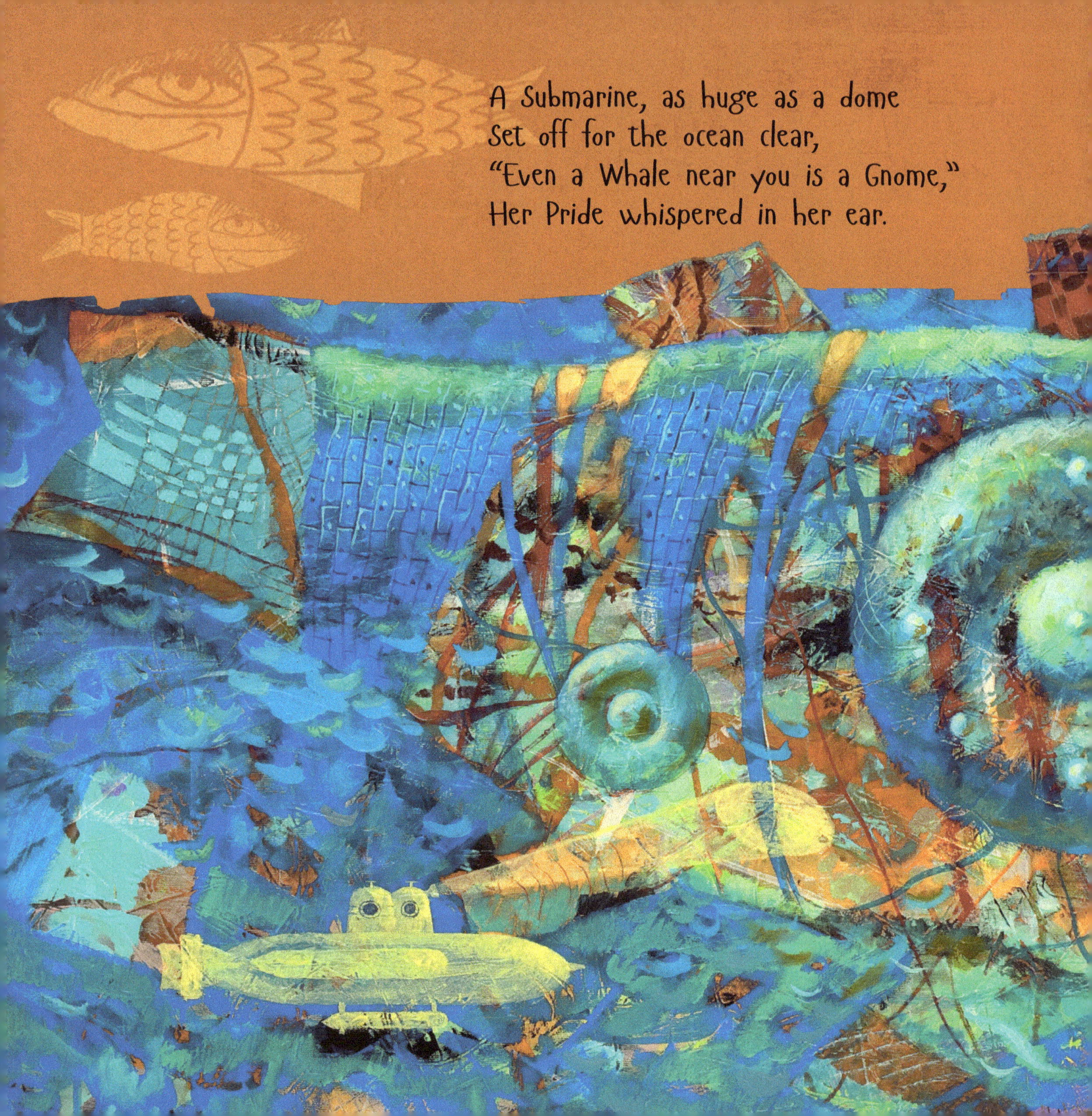

A Submarine, as huge as a dome
Set off for the ocean clear,
"Even a Whale near you is a Gnome,"
Her Pride whispered in her ear.

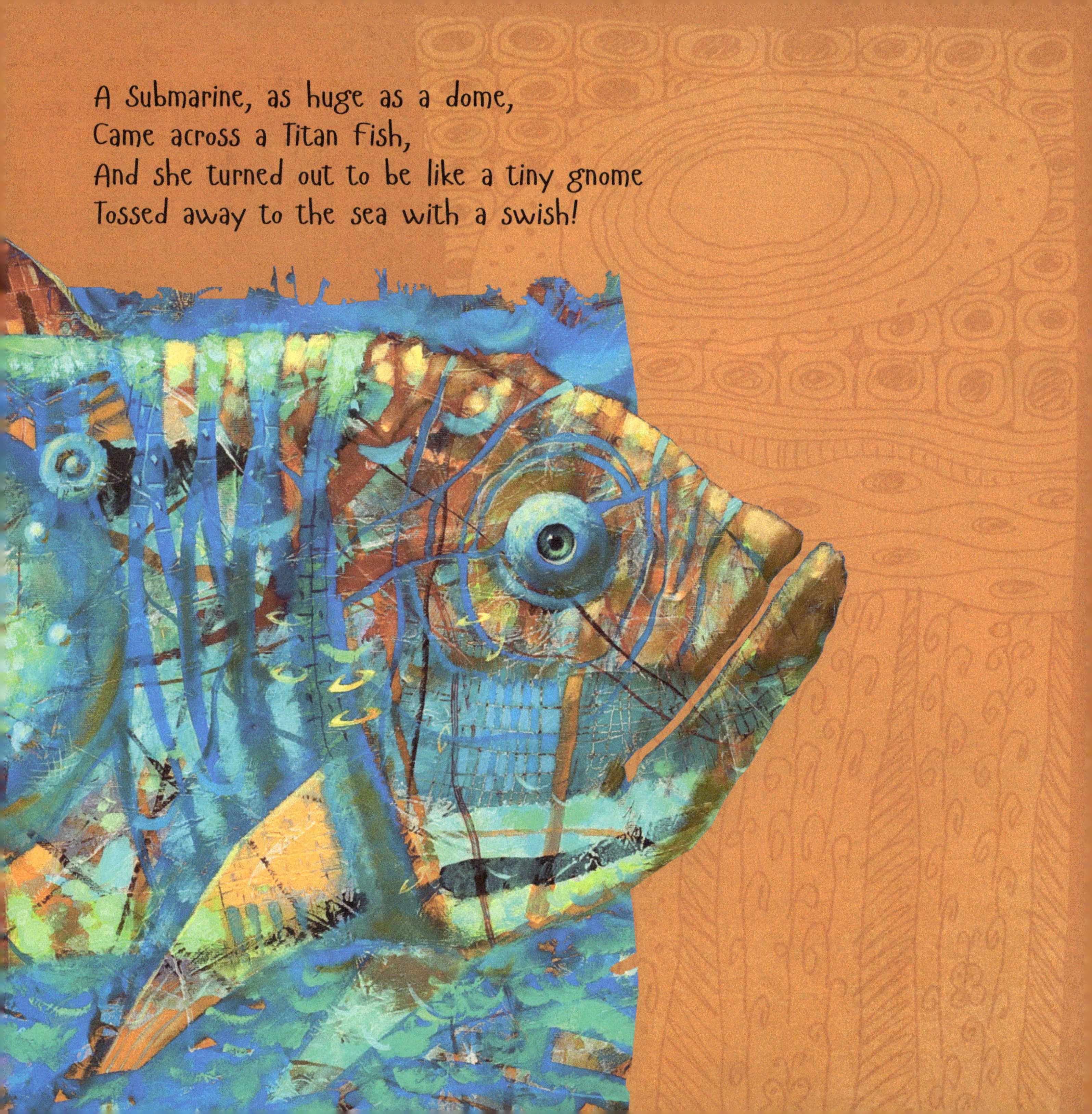

A Submarine, as huge as a dome,
Came across a Titan Fish,
And she turned out to be like a tiny gnome
Tossed away to the sea with a swish!

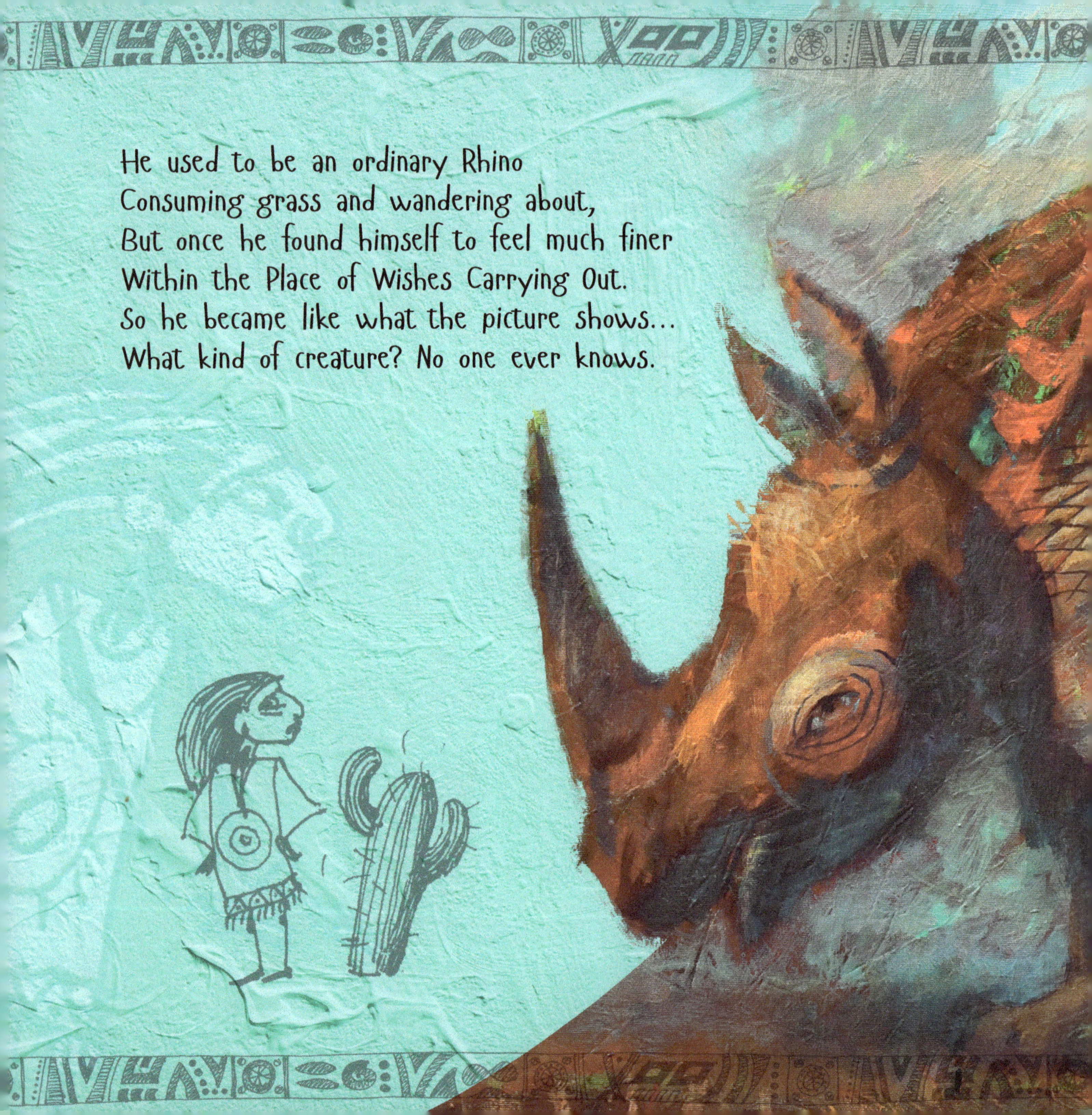

He used to be an ordinary Rhino
Consuming grass and wandering about,
But once he found himself to feel much finer
Within the Place of Wishes Carrying Out.
So he became like what the picture shows...
What kind of creature? No one ever knows.

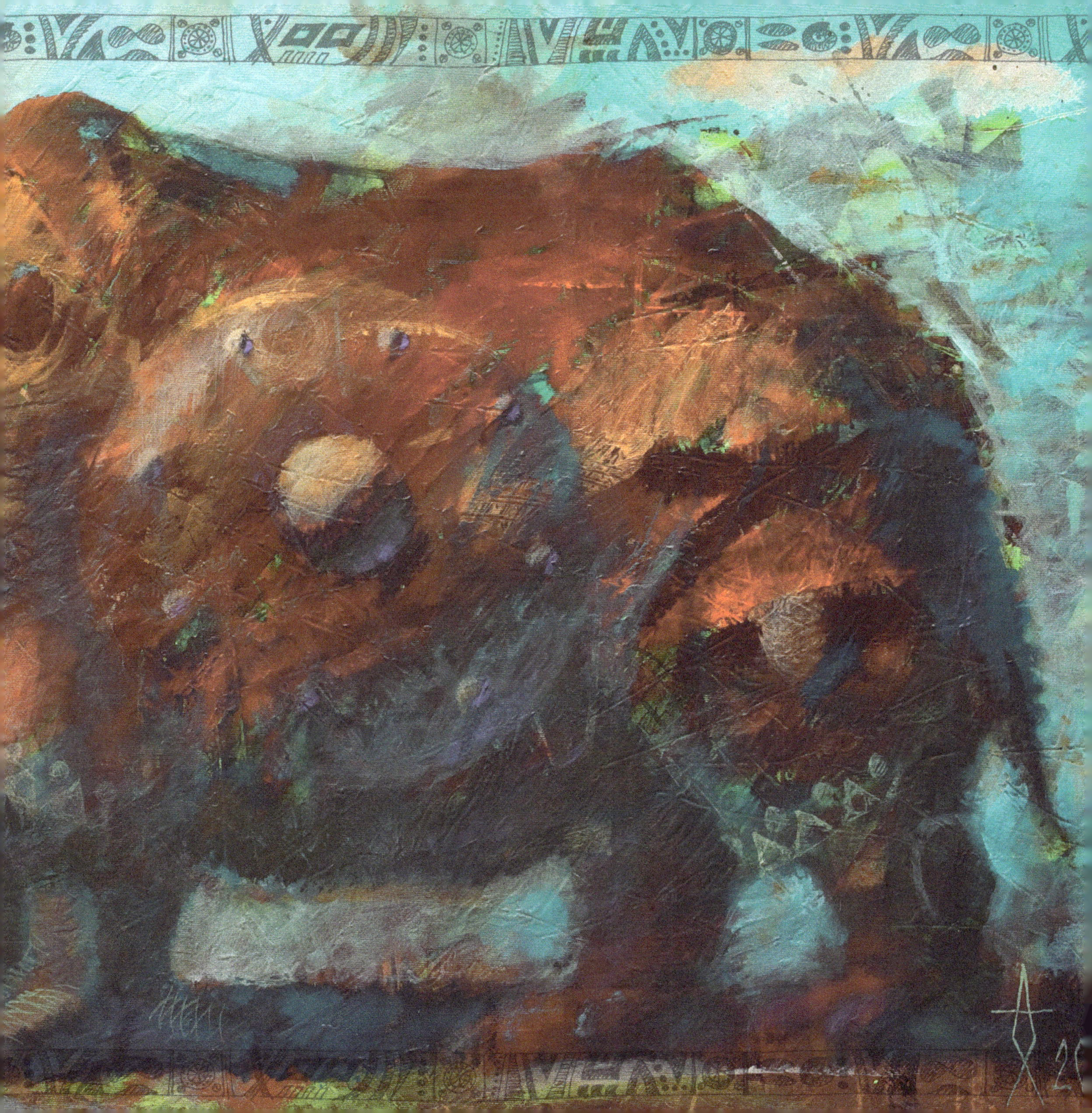

Two giants of different Worlds move again
Through Time and through Space so courageous
The Elephants make their way through the Land,
The Pyramids make theirs through Ages!

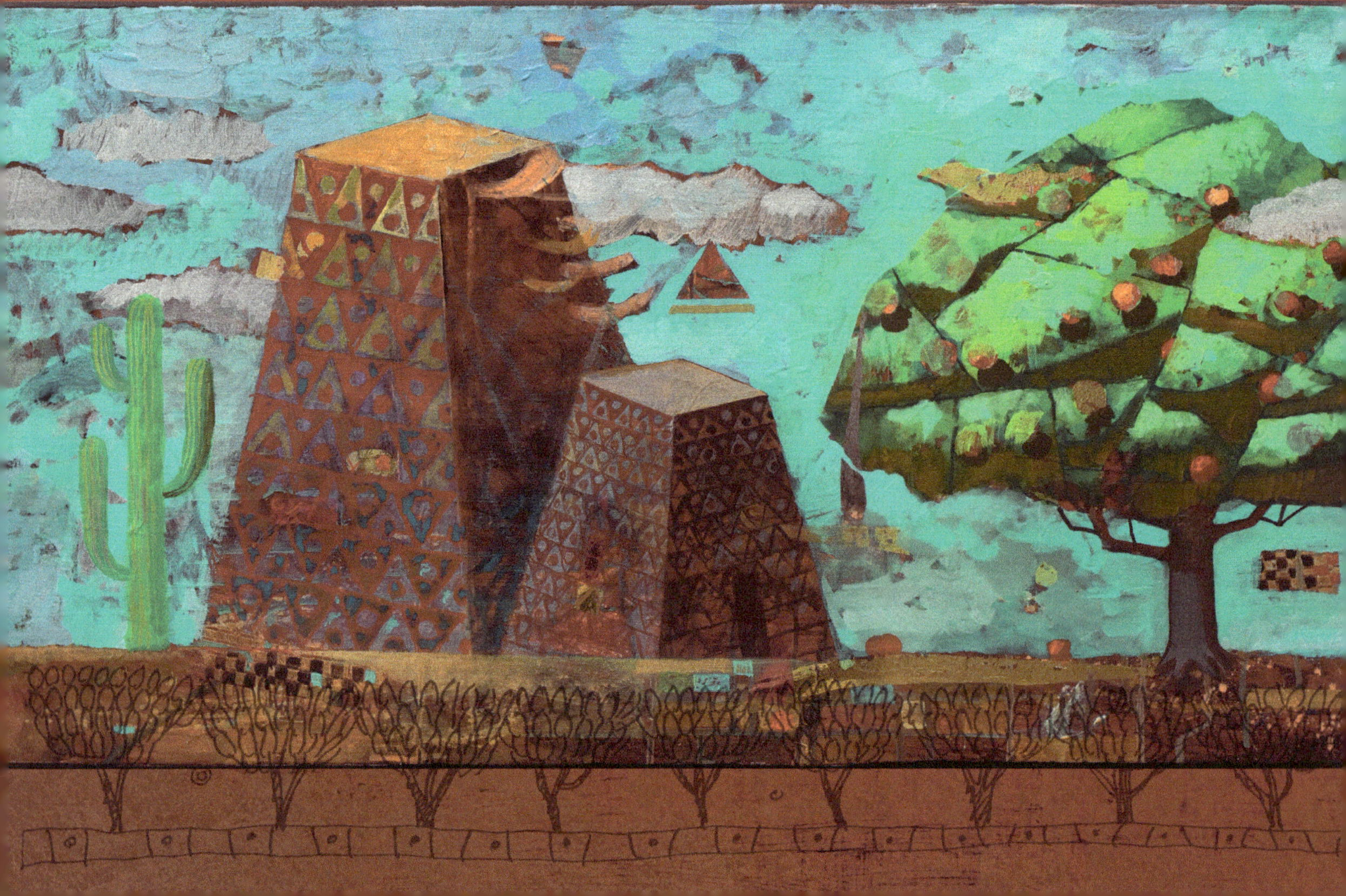

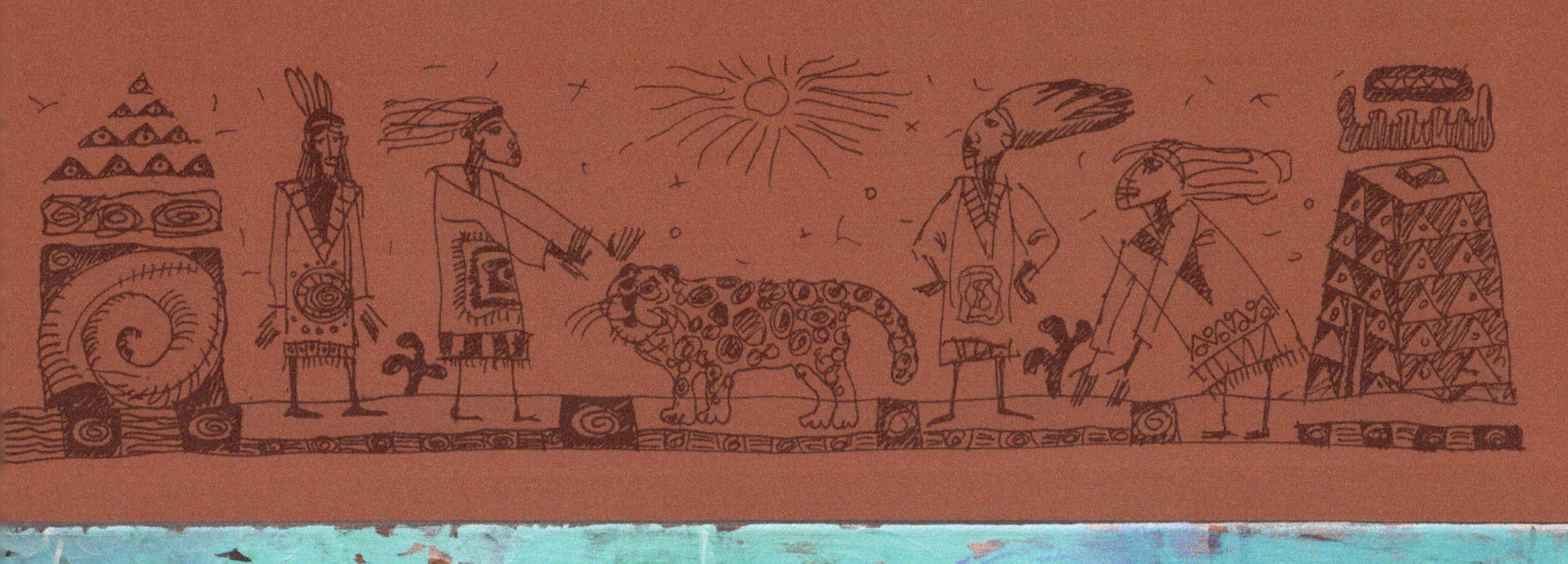

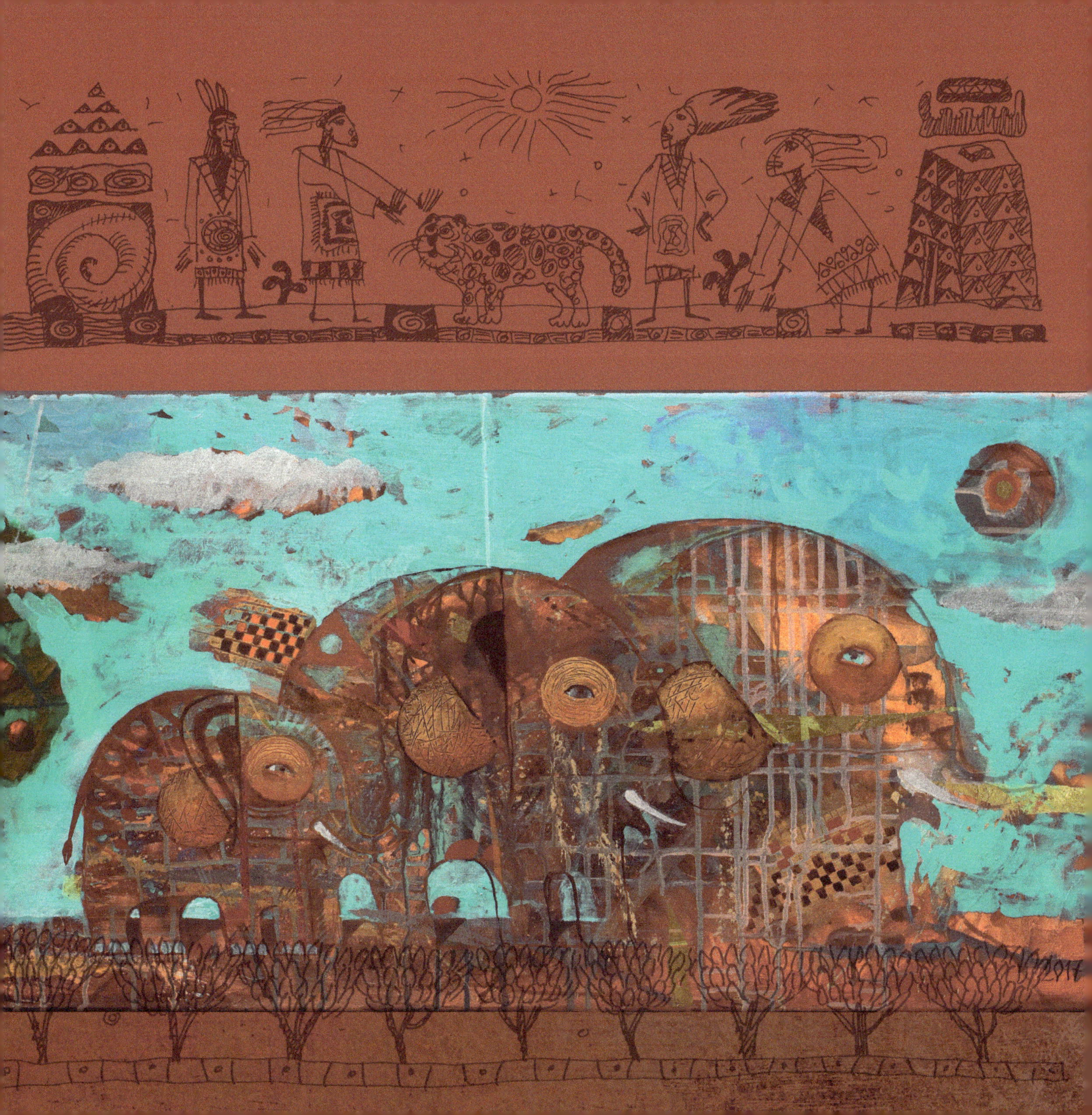

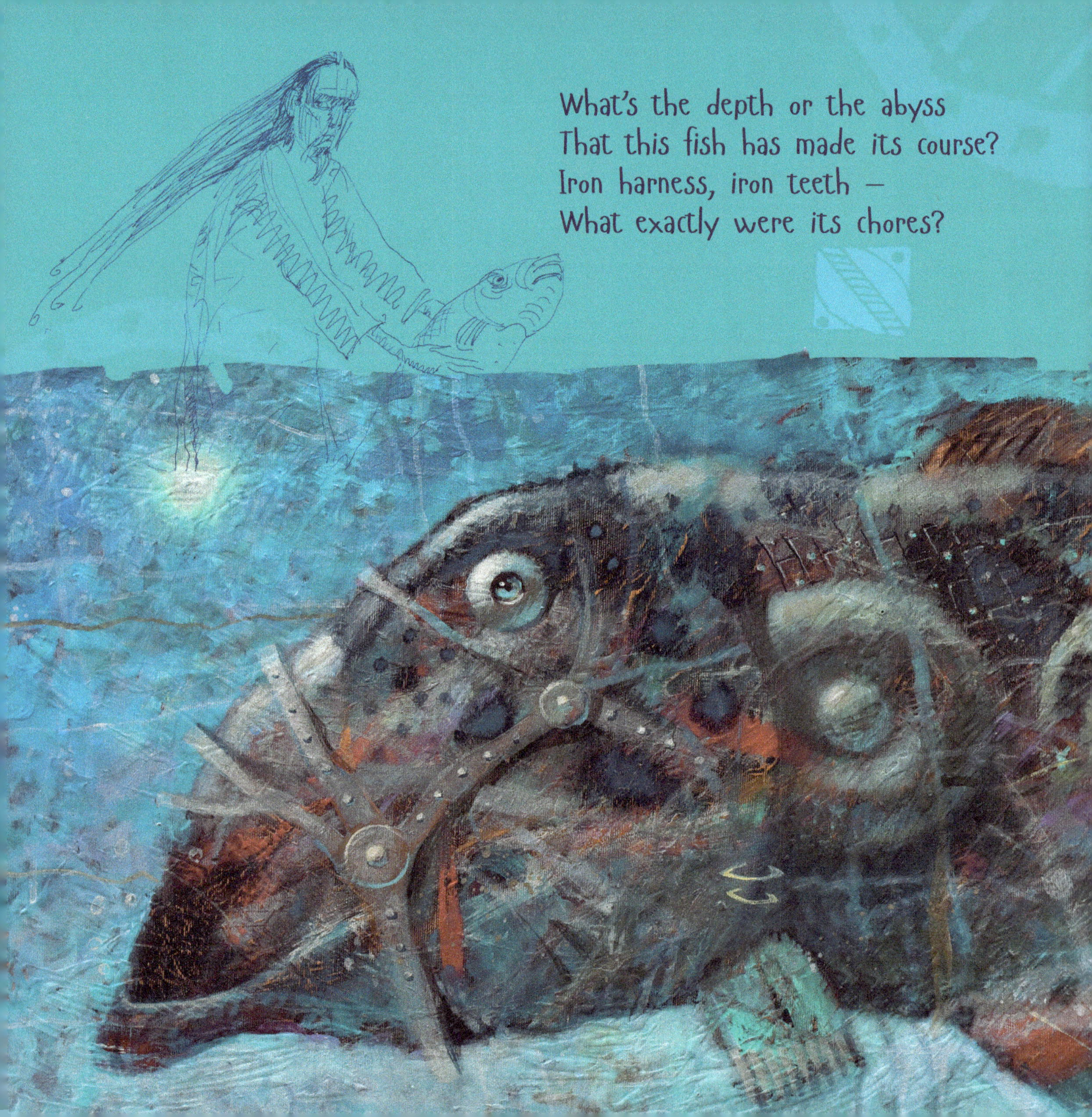

What's the depth or the abyss
That this fish has made its course?
Iron harness, iron teeth —
What exactly were its chores?

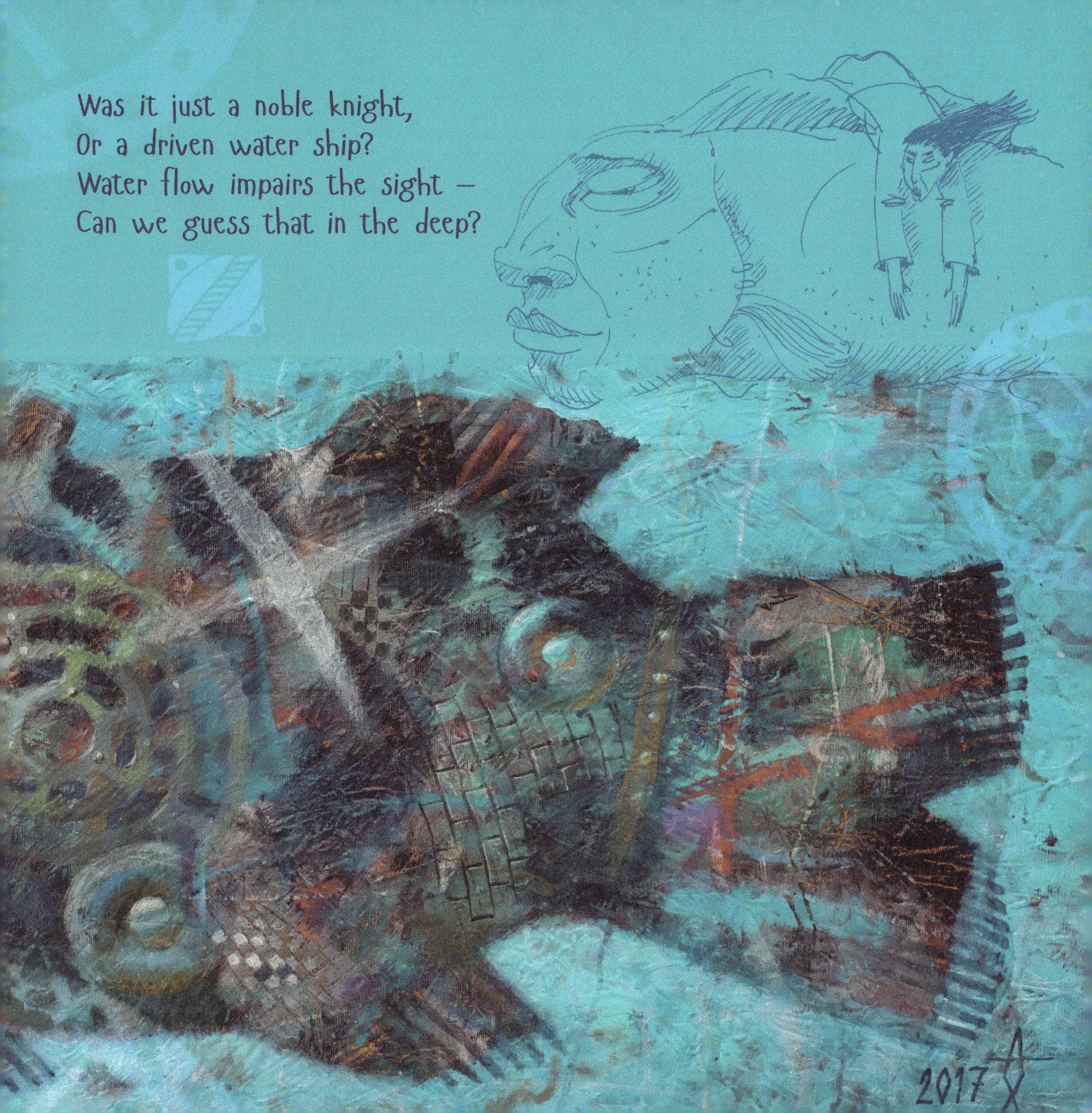
Was it just a noble knight,
Or a driven water ship?
Water flow impairs the sight —
Can we guess that in the deep?

2017

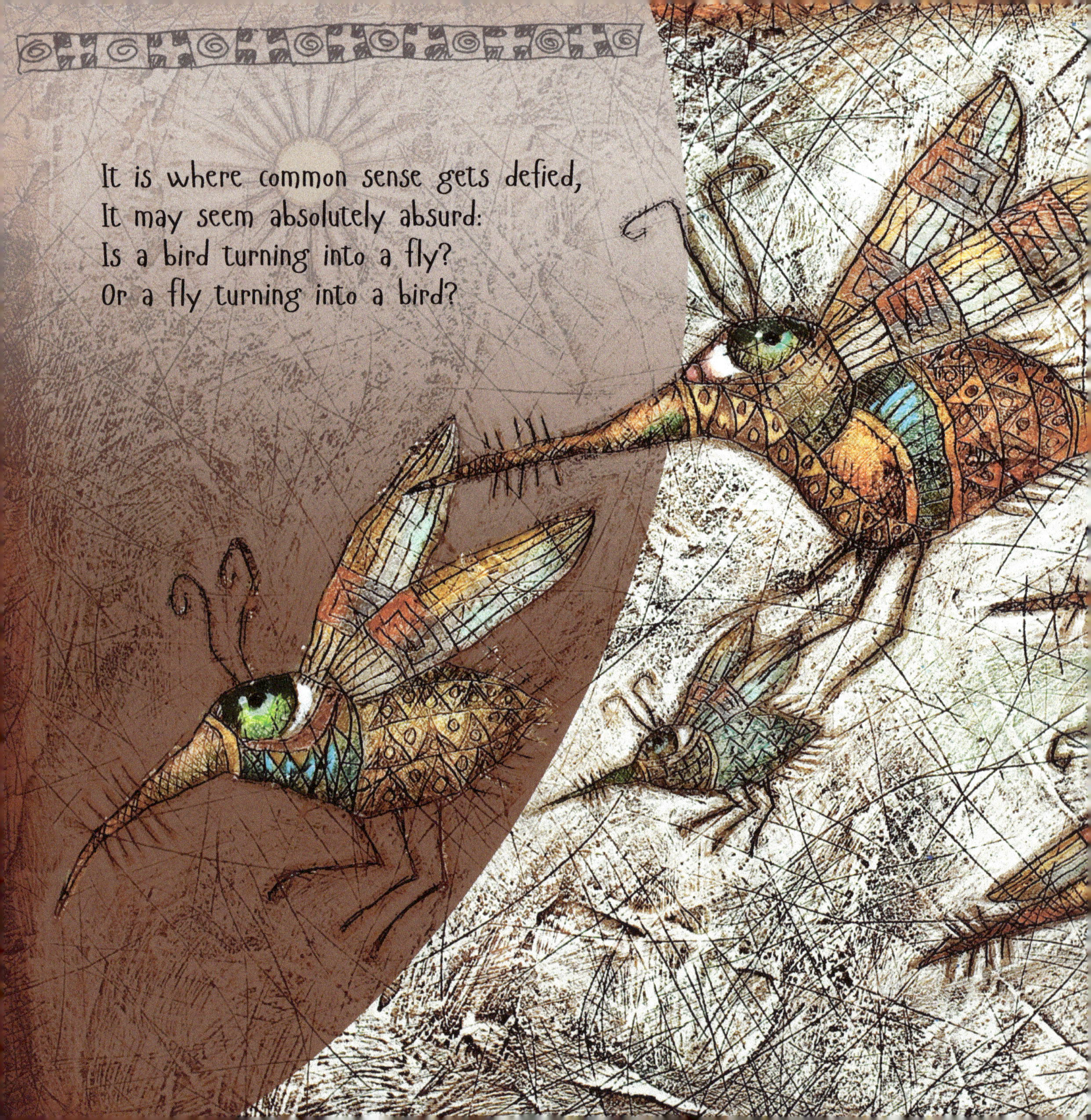

It is where common sense gets defied,
It may seem absolutely absurd:
Is a bird turning into a fly?
Or a fly turning into a bird?

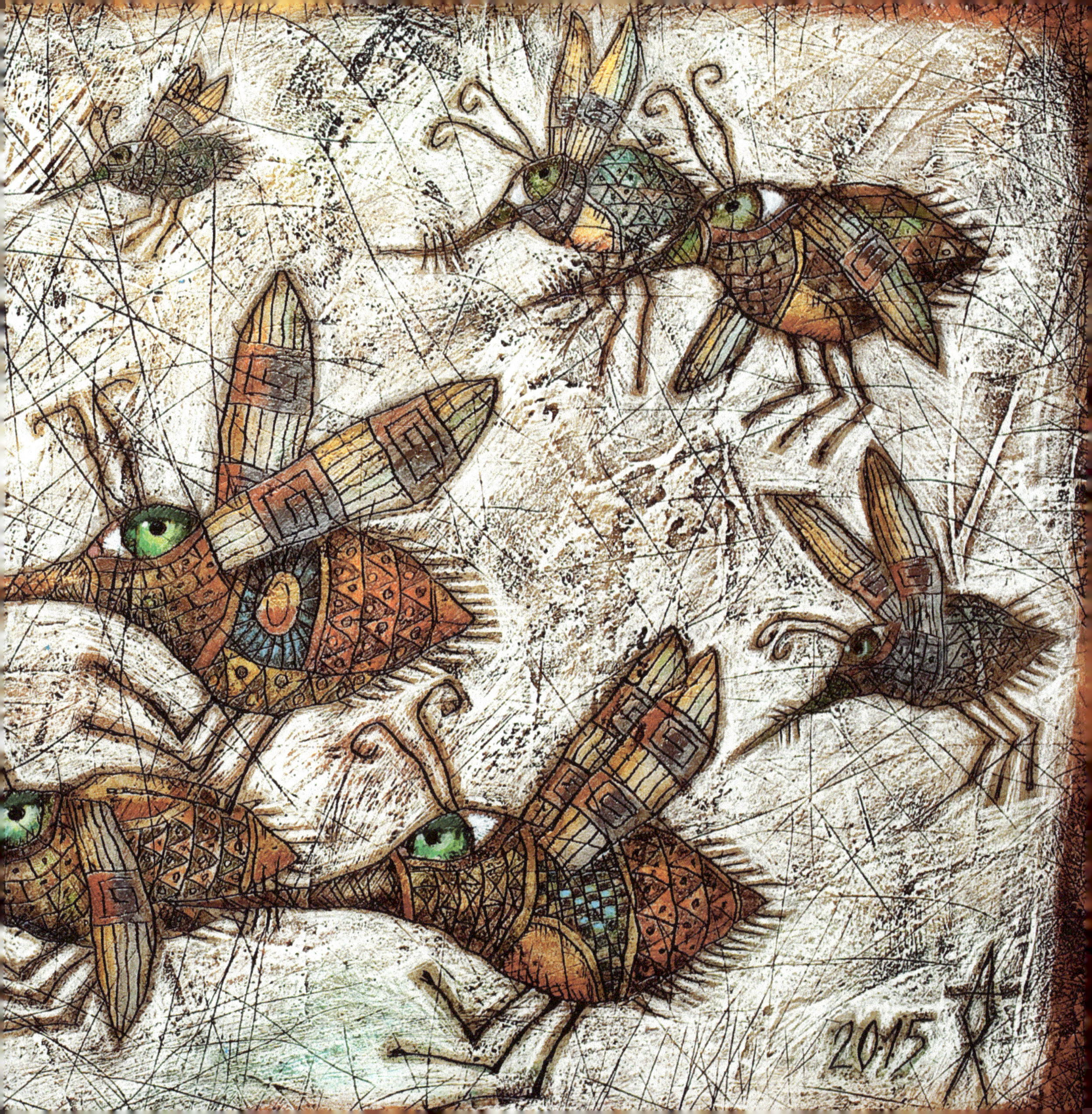
2015

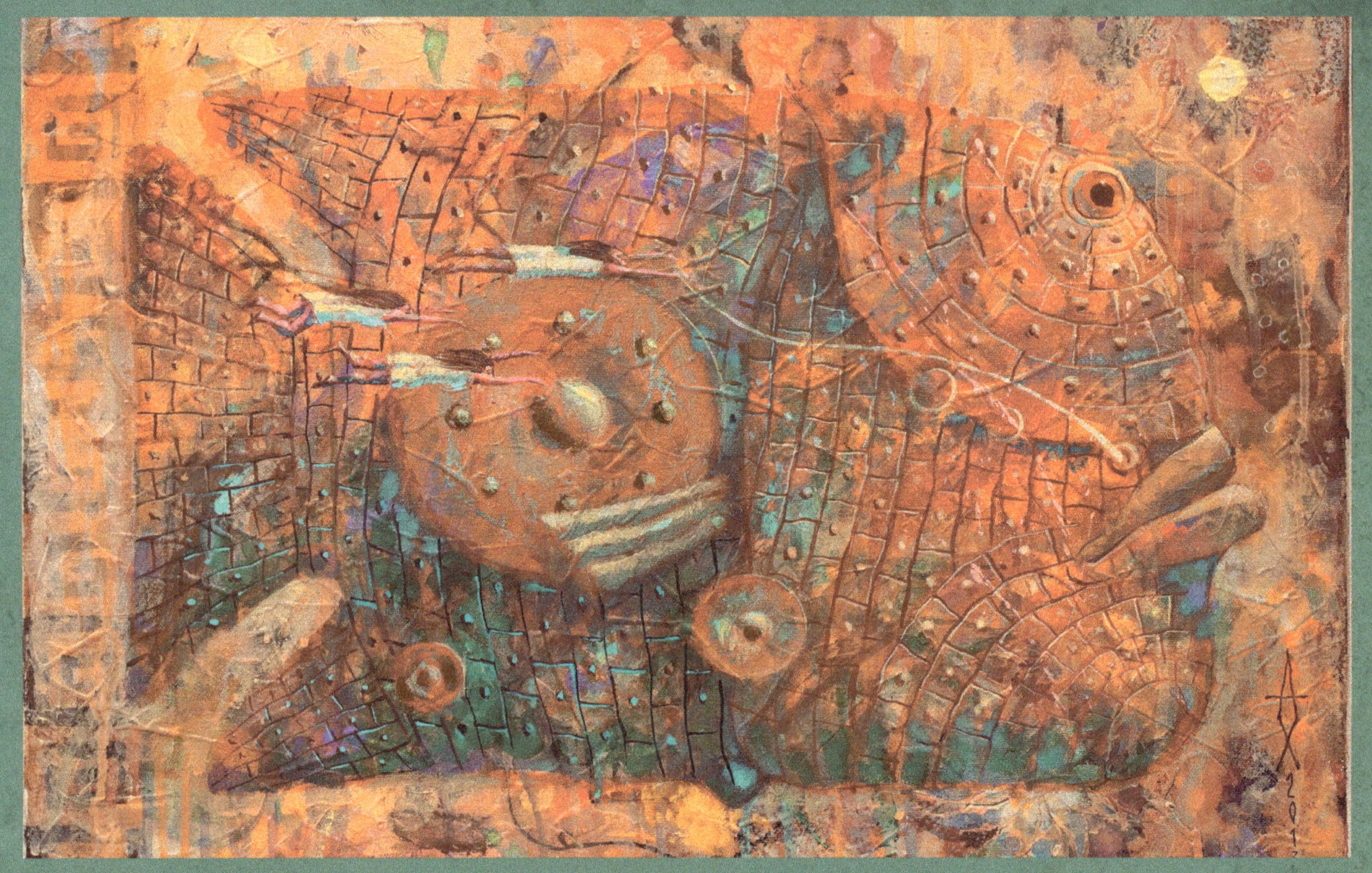

This Fish is a submarine castle,
The abyss brought it up to sight.
Not a king, not a lord nor a vassal —
There is sleeping a noble knight.
Spelled to sleep by an evil Lady
Who had stolen the ancient shield…
And the knight is awaiting the Maiden
That the spell would be sure to yield.
And — Good Heavens! — the Maiden is here!
Even three … so, the spell will be cleared!

A Maya Priest was assured
Creating this Fish for use,
He sang, he danced, he conjured
For fishing to be profuse.
Yet, the History turned its pages,
Putting Mayas in obliteration,
But the Fish keeps swimming through ages
With its wonderful coloration!

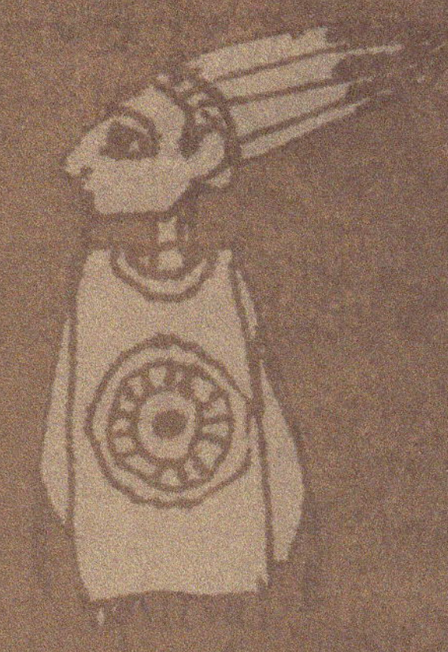

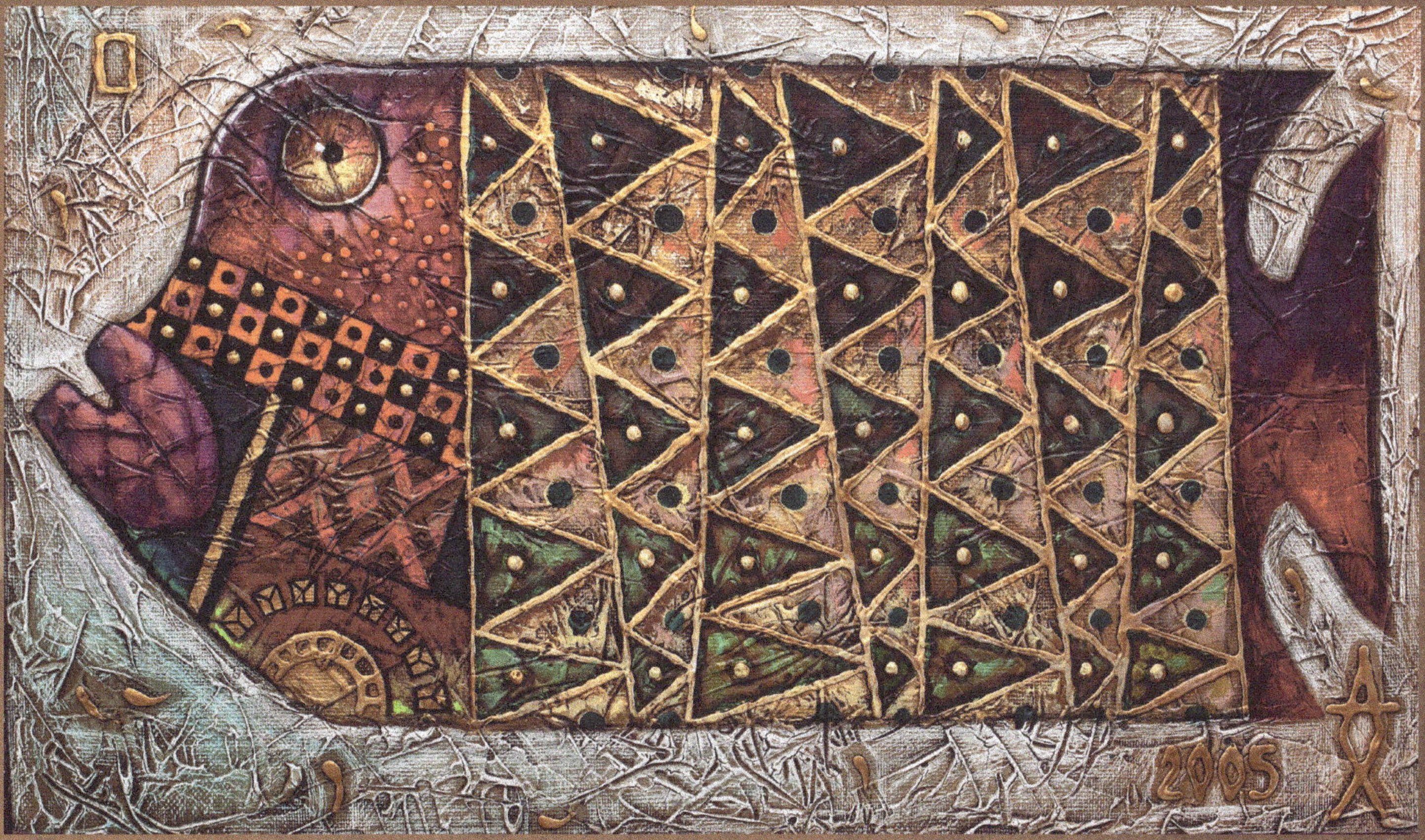

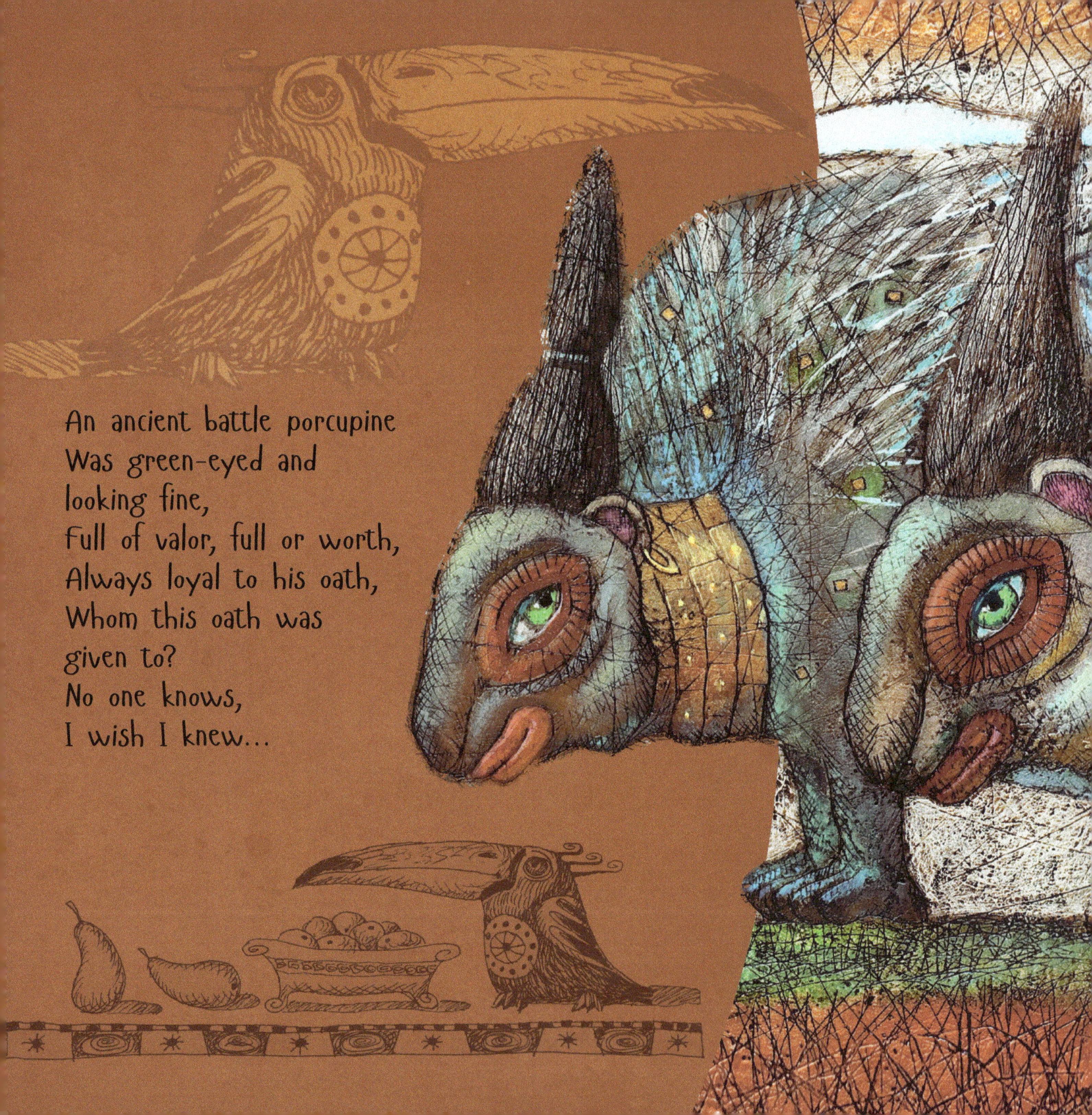

An ancient battle porcupine
Was green-eyed and
looking fine,
Full of valor, full or worth,
Always loyal to his oath,
Whom this oath was
given to?
No one knows,
I wish I knew...

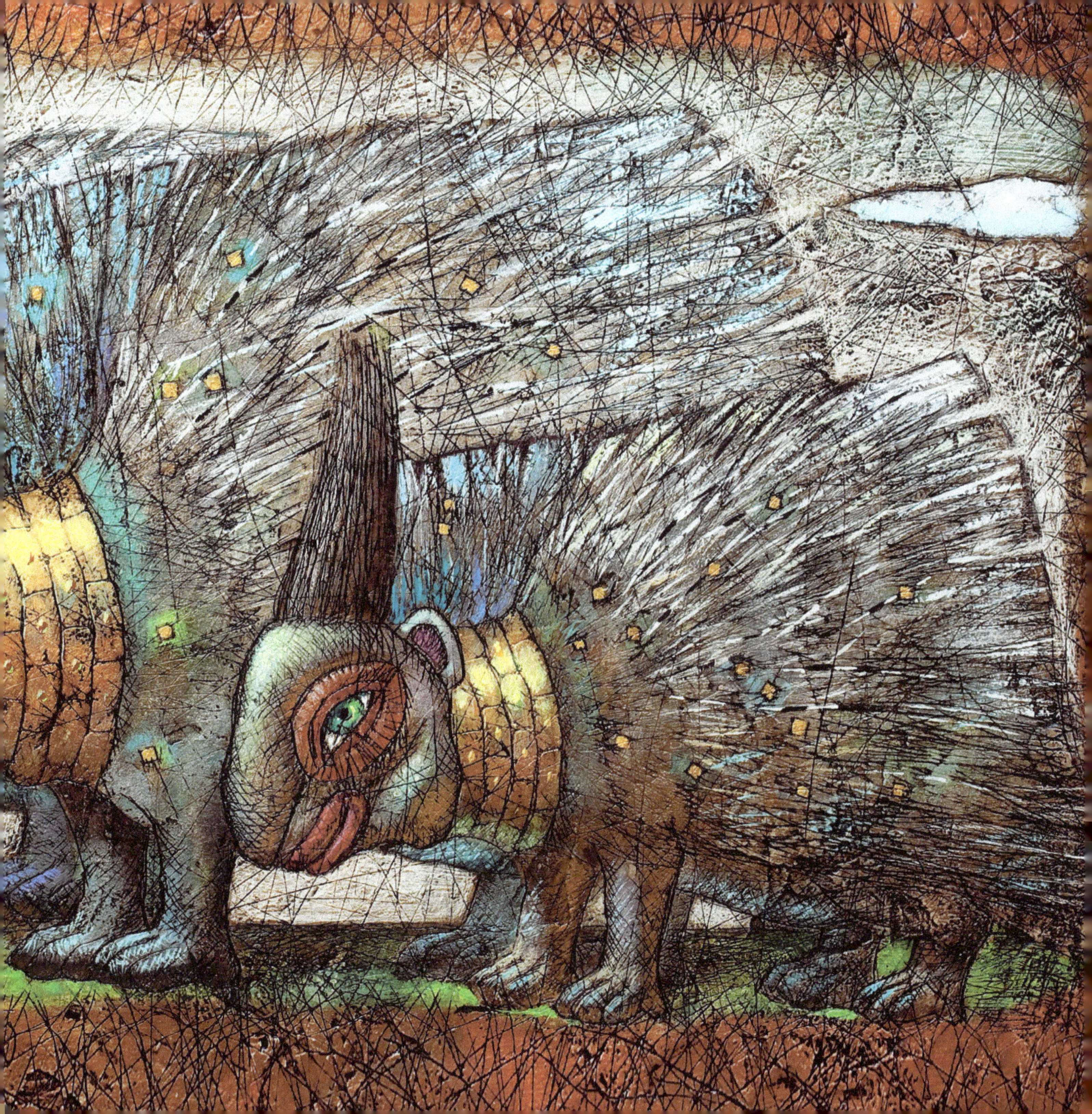

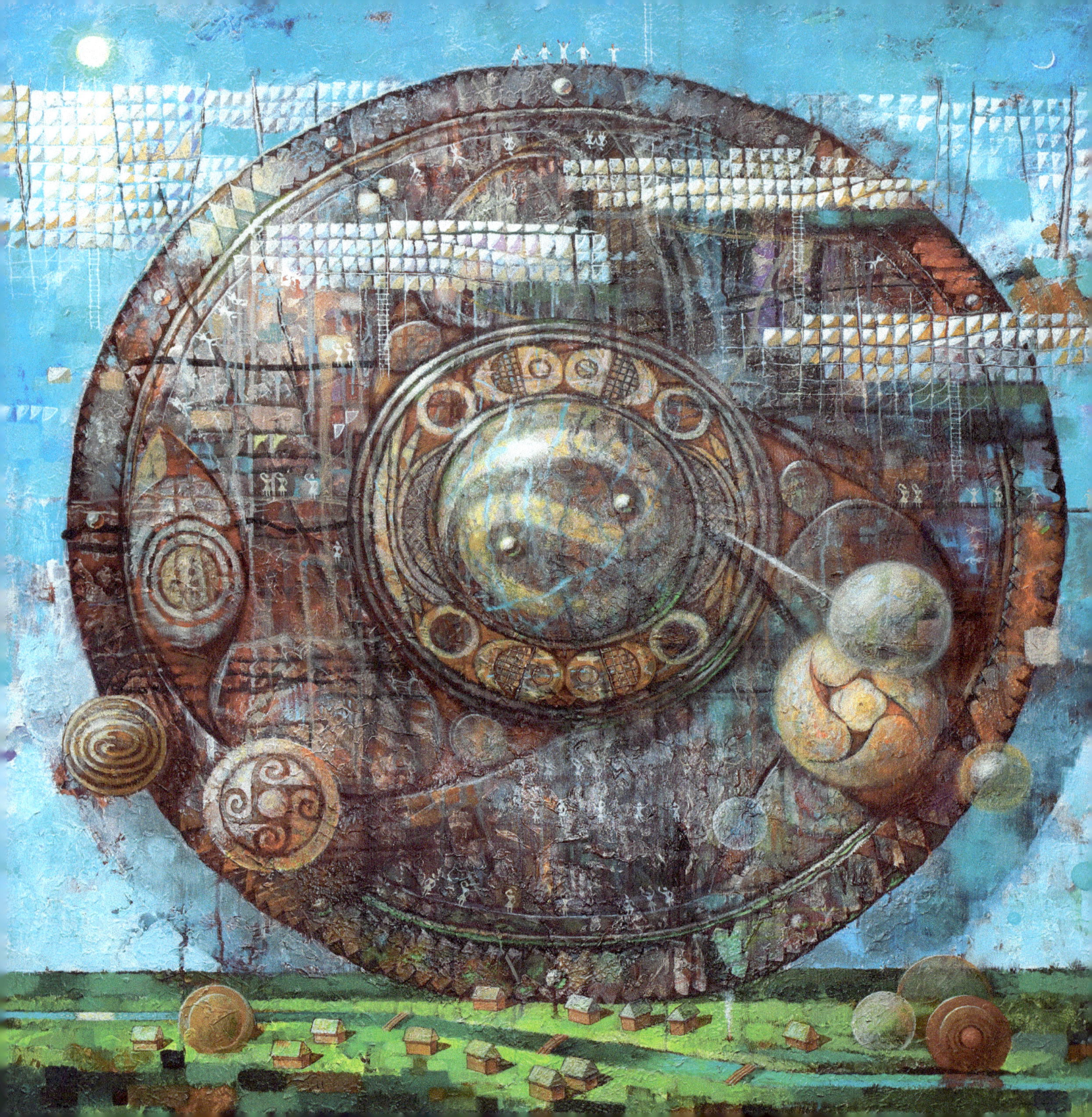

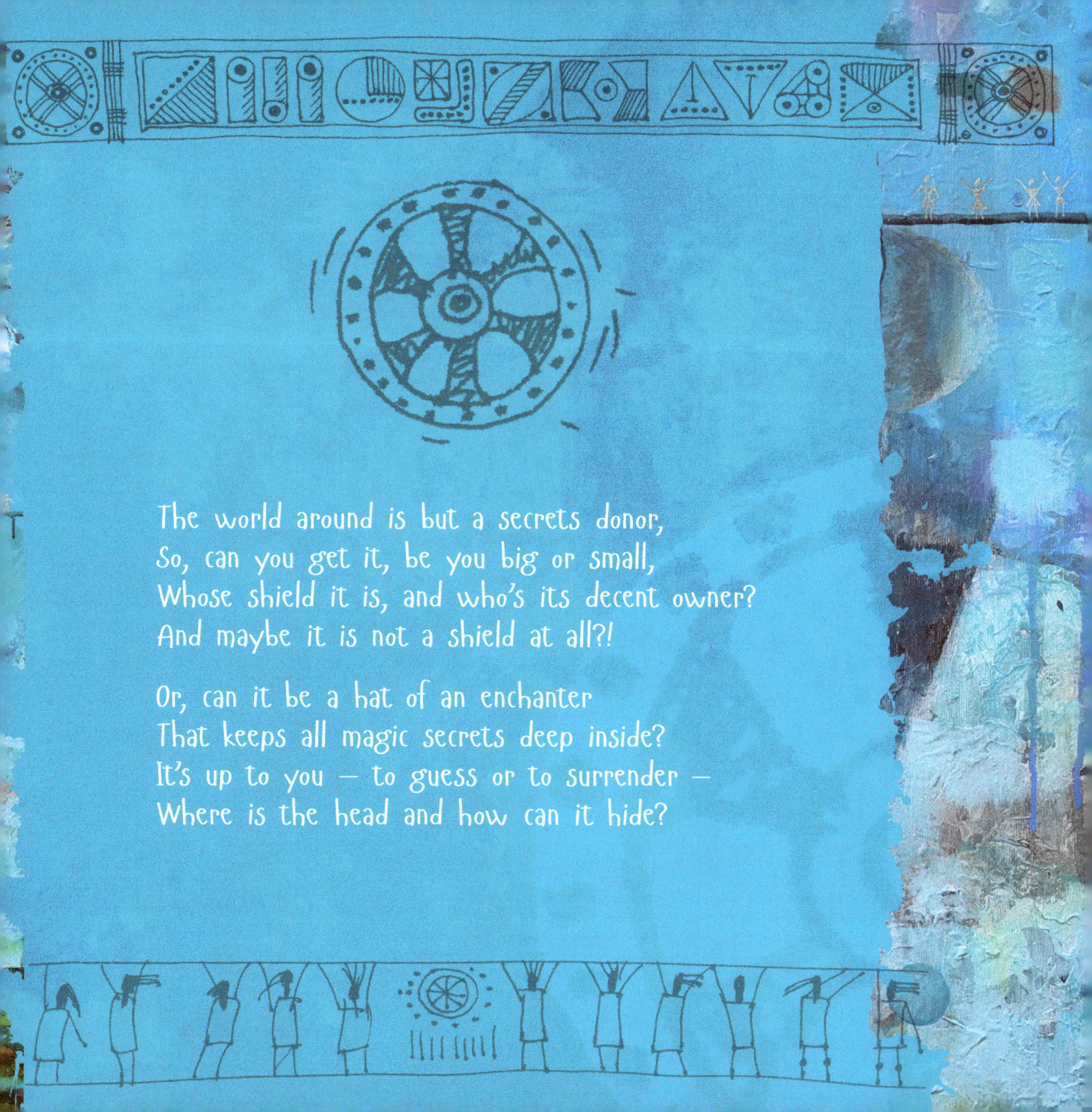

The world around is but a secrets donor,
So, can you get it, be you big or small,
Whose shield it is, and who's its decent owner?
And maybe it is not a shield at all?!

Or, can it be a hat of an enchanter
That keeps all magic secrets deep inside?
It's up to you — to guess or to surrender —
Where is the head and how can it hide?

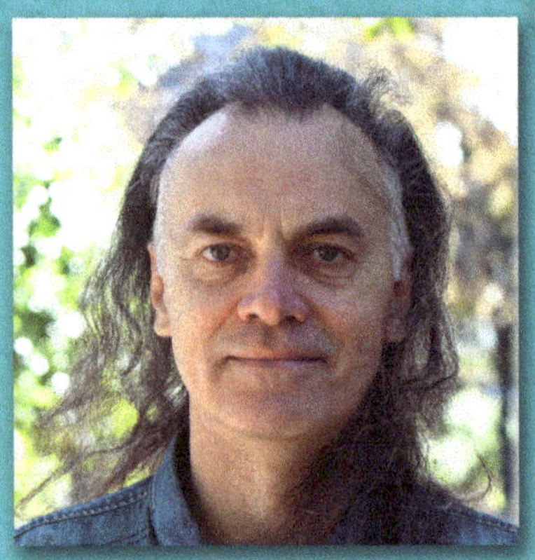

Alexey Khomych

The artist **Alexey Khomych** subtly feels the beauty of the unity of the human and the entire Universe. For the artist, the material and the spiritual are inseparably connected, and it is inside the humans themselves that the holiest and the most insightful can be found. Some of the artist's most valuable creative ideas have been inspired by dreams, which are of great importance for him. www.facebook.com/homich.alexey

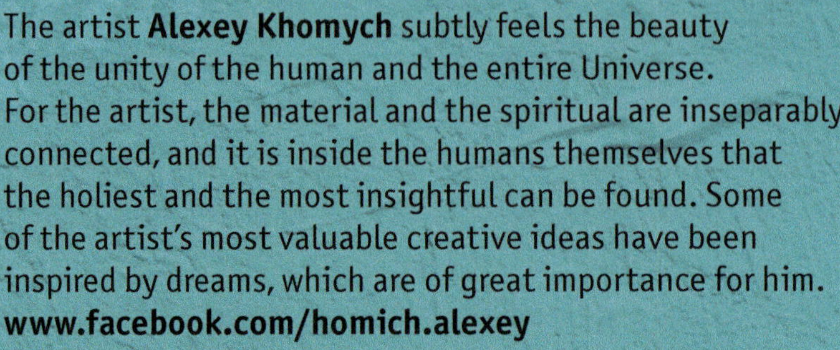

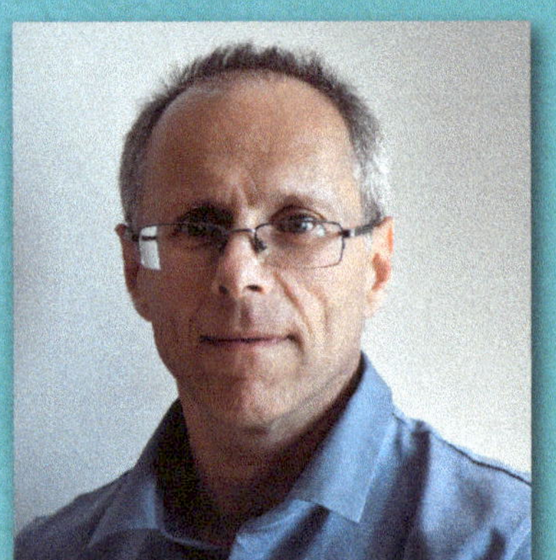

Hennady Malamed

Hennady Malamed is a poet whose works invariably evoke readers' excitement thanks to bright and original humor, puns, and a variety of rhythm.

The genuine sincerity of Hennady's work helps the author to be on the same wavelength with children, thus cultivating their sense of humor and style.

Hennady believes there is some kind of magic in creating poetry, which can't be rendered by words but can only be felt through getting used to good poetry since childhood. It's those magic feelings that readers experience while reading Hennady Malamed's poetry.

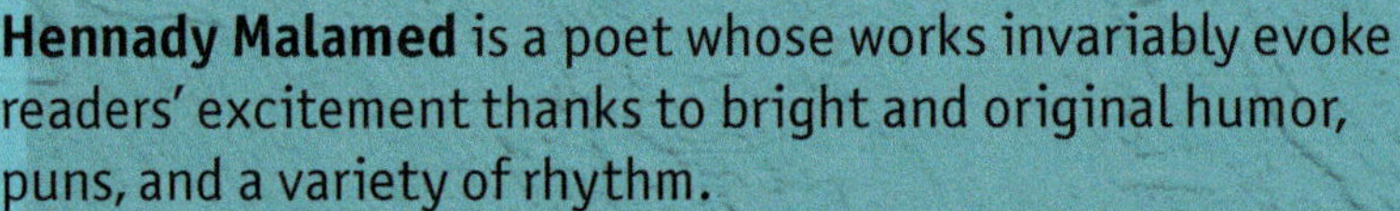

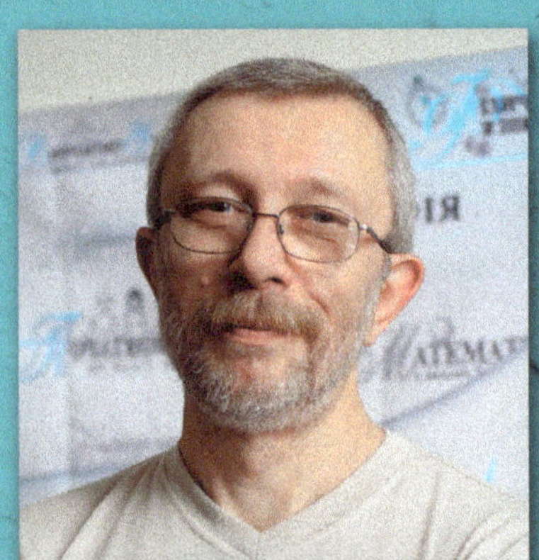

Alexander Lyubchenko

Alexander Lyubchenko has a great experience in ESL teaching, composing and performing music, songwriting, and translating, which combined make his translations a careful and accurate rendering of both the author's original ideas and emotions and the individual style and manner of writing.

Thank you for choosing our book!

You can always find an up-to-date list of the titles of this series as well as our other books, on our FB page:
fb.me/MAGEhut

Subscribe to it! Be the first to know when we have a new release! Sign up for our page to get newsletters. We only post when we have book news — it is true!

Share it! If you enjoyed this book, please lend your copy to a friend who might enjoy it, too.

Review it! Please consider posting a short book review. Honest reader impressions help other people decide whether they might enjoy the book and make the right choice!

Create with us! We'd love to hear from you! Stop by our Facebook page to discuss updates, illustrations, and cover reveals, or just to spend time together!

Love, MAGE team

CPSIA information can be obtained
at www.ICGtesting.com
Printed in the USA
BVHW010242210123
656716BV00010BA/738